pointing dogs

pointing dogs

HOW TO **TRAIN, NURTURE,** AND **APPRECIATE** YOUR **BIRD DOG**

STEVEN MULAK

THE DERRYDALE PRESS
Lanham • Boulder • New York • Toronto • Plymouth, UK

THE DERRYDALE PRESS

Published by The Derrydale Press
An imprint of Rowman & Littlefield
4501 Forbes Boulevard, Suite 200, Lanham, Maryland 20706
www.rowman.com

10 Thornbury Road, Plymouth PL6 7PP, United Kingdom

Distributed by National Book Network

British Library Cataloguing in Publication Information Available

Library of Congress Cataloging-in-Publication Data
The hardback edition of this book was previously cataloged by the
Library of Congress as follows:

Mulak, Steven J.
Pointing dogs made easy: how to train, nurture, and appreciate your bird dog /
by Steven Mulak: foreword by Mark C. Dilts. —
1st ed.
p. cm.
1. Bird dogs—Training. 2. Pointers (Dogs) I. Title.
SF428.5.M84   1995
636.7'0886—dc20   95-31114

ISBN: 978-1-58667-130-3 (pbk. : paper)
ISBN: 978-1-58667-131-0 (electronic)

∞™ The paper used in this publication meets the minimum requirements of
American National Standard for Information Sciences—Permanence of
Paper for Printed Library Materials, ANSI/NISO Z39.48-1992.

Printed in the United States of America

For Susan,
more lovely than I ever dreamed

Contents

Foreword

Forewords are as different as the people who write them. Their intended purpose, however, remains the same. They are meant to give you a reason for reading the book in which they appear. In this case, my task has been made quite easy by the fact that this book has been written by Steven J. Mulak. To those acquainted with his work, no more need be said. To others, further explanation is in order.

I became aware of Steven Mulak when I was editing a magazine more than a decade ago. The morning mail had brought, in addition to the usual letters, bills, and advertisements, a large manila envelope containing the literary efforts of a young, aspiring writer whose talent was as obvious as his eagerness to tell his story.

It happened that his story was too long for us to use, so, bowing to Steven's request in his cover letter accompanying the manuscript, I wrote to him suggesting what he might do to make the article acceptable to us. Receipt of my letter prompted a telephone call from him to discuss the revisions. We talked of many things and, thus, began a lasting friendship.

During the subsequent ten years, we have hunted twittering timberdoodles in beautiful Vermont woodcock covers; been chilled to the bone hunting waterfowl; and shared steaming coffee and donuts with his father in a salt marsh. We've stumbled and fallen in the rushing water of a wilderness river while chasing Maine's wary Atlantic salmon together. I shared his sorrow the day his setter made the trip to the veterinarian and never returned. And I stood in his tidy garage as he told me of the deer mouse that, much to the chagrin of his lovely wife, had taken up housekeeping in the woodpile. We've had some great times together, the kind that only friends can share and enjoy to the fullest. All without having ever met face to face.

You see, Steven has that unique ability (coveted by all serious writers) to select just the right picturesque word or colorful description that will enhance the scene he is painting for his readers. It is this finely honed talent, this wonderful ability to transfer feelings and keen observations to the written page, that makes us nod our heads in silent recognition, as if we too have witnessed the scene he has described to us. His writing—much like Steven himself—is intelligent, honest, enthusiastic, insightful, humorous, and always down to earth. He can put tears in your eyes and a lump in your throat one moment and have you chuckling aloud the next.

Although we worked together and corresponded frequently (both by telephone and mail) since becoming acquainted in 1976, it wasn't until late 1987 that I had the pleasure of meeting him. During the intervening years, I have marveled at his professional growth, admired his determination, and have developed a deep and abiding envy of his vast array of skills (He is a champion decoy carver and a fine illustrator—of both this and his previous book, *Brown Feathers*). He is, in my humble opinion, one of the most skilled storytellers in the outdoor-writing field. I am certain that after you have read this, his latest book, you will agree with my appraisal.

Mark C. Dilts

Preface

I guess if I had to blame anyone, it would be Lee Wulff. He's the one responsible for all this.

Here I was, a kid with typical teenage ideas and dreams about Corvettes and penny loafers and all other things that came under the heading of *cool*. Then, one late-summer evening my father and I went to a sportsmen's spaghetti supper at the local American Legion post. Lee Wulff and his pretty wife were there answering questions and demonstrating a new method of teaching fly fishing that involved yarn rather than fly line.

Then they showed a movie. In it, Lee Wulff was using Winchester products and hunting game birds in various parts of the country. When they got to the quail hunting sequence, it happened: On the screen appeared a pair of English pointers that did something I had never seen before—they pointed birds. Now, my dad owned a Brittany spaniel back then, and I'm sure that his dog at one time or another did something that could be interpreted as "pointing birds."

But not like *that*.

The English pointers in that film seemed aware of their own gracefulness as they crept into pointing postures. They held tight, even after the covey flushed. And, unlike our dog, they didn't have to be chased down and strong-armed before surrendering the birds they fetched. For me, the manners and intensity of those pointers in the movie might have been something from outer space. I hadn't even suspected such things existed.

It was a classic case of love at first sight.

This was the early 1960s. Back then, fifty dollars bought a secondhand Remington pumpgun. A good pair of boots would run you fifteen. Paperback books were fifty or sixty cents, and you could mail a letter for a nickel. The pointers that held my fascination were referred to as "thousand-dollar dogs," or, in my mind anyway, the kind that you had to mortgage the house to buy.

Money was no problem—I didn't have any. But I was still young and foolish enough to believe there was nothing I couldn't do if I put enough effort into it. Way back in my mind something whispered, "If you want a dog like that badly enough, you can *make your own*."

I've been trying ever since.

Acknowledgments

There are a number of people mentioned in this book. Here's a little more about them.

Susan is at the top of the list because she has put up with me for a long time without complaining very much. After twenty-six years, she still laughs at my jokes. That's got to count for something.

My father doesn't hunt anymore, but I get chewed out if I don't call him and tell him how things went. The best compliment people can pay to me is to compare me to Dad. He's widely thought of as a nice guy, so that doesn't happen very often. He's seventy-five.

Frank Roach is a professional dog trainer from the Texas Panhandle town of Pampa. He is among the most generous men I have ever met. He claims to be retired, but still has a lot of dogs that belong to other people in his kennels.

Colonel Sam Paul is retired and lives in Chicopee where he trains dogs, hunts hard, and golfs in the high seventies. When asked in which branch of the military he served, his reply is always, "the infantry." I admire that sort of loyalty.

Mark Dilts wrote the foreword when I first mentioned this book to him. He is the man who got me started in the writing business, and I always thought of him as my mentor—with all the term implies. He died in 1994.

Bill Puza was from Westfield, Massachusetts. He was a gentleman and a gentle man. I wish I could have known him longer. He died in the late 1980s.

Tommy Lamica was a friend who made a lasting impression on everyone who knew him. He had a remarkable way with bird dogs. He died a young man in 1985, but continues to make appearances in my stories.

Eric Mulak lives on Cape Cod, where he works as an appraiser for an auction house. It would be foolish to bet against him in any endeavor requiring the use of a shotgun.

Tekoa Mountain Hazel pointed her first grouse on November 1, 1979 and her last on November 29, 1989. In between she pointed 408 others. She was the answer to every prayer I ever prayed for a bird dog.

Wonsover Amy, in her spare time, lives in the back yard with my other setters. At an age when other dogs have long since outgrown the game, she still creeps up on robins and mourning doves, pointing solely for the hell of it. She is the embodiment of the pointing addiction, and I envy her the singularity of her life's work.

Don't stand there and jaw at the dog—
Show him what you want him to do. If the dog
could understand all that yelling, you wouldn't
have to spend time trainin' him—You could
just leave him a note.

        Frank Roach, dog pro
        Pampa, Texas

There are no mistakes—only lessons.

        Message in a Chinese fortune cookie
        Su's Restaurant, Westfield, Massachusetts

The Top Ten Lessons We Learn From Bird Dogs

On a lovely but cold November morning, Dad and I sat taking a break on the truck's tailgate. It was just after ten o'clock, and the cooler contained two pheasants we had taken. In the distance, a hunter stood in a field hollering at his dog. We sipped our coffee and watched the show.

The man alternately ordered his dog to "Get in here!" then switched to descriptions of what he was going to do when he got hold of Sparky. Profanity seemed to be the man's strong suit.

On the receiving end was a typical Saturday morning dog—a big running setter with a merry tail and lots of energy. And, like most other Saturday morning dogs, Sparky seemed completely unimpressed by his master's orders and threats. As he bounded, I'm certain his thoughts were along the lines of, "This guy of mine is obviously no philosopher; everybody knows birds gotta fly, fish gotta swim, and dogs gotta run."

Ultimately, when he had investigated everything that had kept him running, Sparky went in to see what his master was yelling about. Only then did the man beat the tar out of the him.

Now think about it. As long as Sparky was ignoring his handler, nothing bad happened to him. But as soon as he obeyed his master's command ("Get in here!") he got beat up. As Dad pointed out, one needn't be a Sesame Street graduate to answer this one: *What did man teach dog?*

Dogs are born with potential, but good dogs are made. Ol' Sparky might have been the pick of the litter out of a well-bred line of quality setters, but let's face it, he was not going to teach himself to be obedient.

Unfortunately, neither was his owner.

Instead, that chowderhead seemed intent on embodying all the mistakes that might be made in training a dog—sort of a find-the-ten-things-wrong-with-this-picture exercise come to life.

There are no mistakes—only lessons. When I read that in a fortune cookie twenty years ago, it hit me just right. The idea, of course, is founded in the truism that we must all learn from our mistakes. After half a lifetime of working with bird dogs, I can tell you that (by fortune cookie definition) I've personally received a *lot* of lessons. In my compulsion to quantify everything, I made up a list of the top ten most common lessons my dogs have taught me. See how many you recognize.

1. So waddya want from me?

By far, the most common mistake made by first-time bird dog owners is not knowing what they want the dog to do. They have unknown expectations. Oh, they might say,

"I want him to find birds," or, "I want him to hunt."

Sure. Me too.

But let's get specific. How far away do you want him to be when he finds those birds? And what do you want him to do once he's found them? Do you want him to point? Retrieve? What sort of manners must he have? Will he do these things by himself, or are you going to have to teach him? And how are you, the trainer, going to go about turning him into the dog you want him to become?

The key question has to be: *How much dog do you want?* For most of us, the right answer lies somewhere between the perfection of the U.S. National Amateur Shooting Dog champion and the opposite extreme—those untrained bird dogs that can been seen running amuck at public shooting areas.

As a dog man, my father had very low expectations—he was always happy if his dog stayed within gun range and would find pheasants that were trying hard not to be found. Anything else was gravy. I might add that he was almost always happy with his dogs.

Perhaps your standards are higher. You might want a dog that points and retrieves and knows enough to do his business outside, but maybe things like being rock-steady to the gun and backing another dog on sight are things that don't mean a great deal to you. Understand, too, that there is a world of difference (read: "a huge amount of training") be-tween a dog that points *most* of the birds he finds and one that *points them all.* The currency in dog training is time, and  you can find out just how good you want Sparky to be by figuring out how much of that currency you're willing to spend on him.

What should you do?

Join a bird dog club. Go to a few field trials. Ask questions of people who have the sort of dog you'd like to own. Establish a list of things that are and are not important to you. A family meeting in which everyone can agree on what and what not to do in training the dog is a good start, especially if the dog is to be a family pet as well as your hunting partner. What's our plan for housebreaking the dog? If he's allowed in the house, where is he permitted and not permitted to go? What do we do when he barks?

So make your list. If you have a good idea of what you want your dog to become and a plan for getting him there, you've avoided the most common mistake of amateur bird dog owners. The actual nuts and bolts of training are something else, but with a plan and a goal, you're on your way.

Confession is supposed to be good for the soul. Here's mine: I was a young man, and had just started working with my second Brittany. At a dog club meeting I took to heart a statement by an experienced dog trainer. What he said was something along the lines of, "I wouldn't have a dog in my kennel that wouldn't back on sight."

I knew that it's a smart man who believes only half of what he hears, and it's a wise man who knows which half to believe. I knew that, but I wasn't wise. Instead, I was just unsure of myself enough to take him at his word. After all, this guy had been at the game for years, and he should have known what he was talking about. I temporarily abandoned my attempts to get my new Brittany to quarter, and instead worked on something that, in truth, is a very minor form of manners, something that only becomes important in specific situations.

The happy part of this story is that only a few weeks passed before I happened to be at a club field trial and had an opportunity to observe the expert's dogs. Not only were they runaways, but they didn't back, either.

In your own training, I hope you will be wise and realize that the only things your dog should do are those things that are important to you, not to someone else.

2. Why do you have to treat me like a dog?

Whenever I talk obedience, someone always says, "I would make him do that, but it would mean coming down hard on the dog, and I don't want to *break his spirit*."

Now, I'll admit that "not breaking the dog's spirit" sounds like the sort of thing you can hang your hat on. But if a dog's spirit was such a delicate thing that discipline would break it, then being imprisoned in a kennel for days at a time would absolutely destroy it.

It isn't, and it doesn't.

The truly good bird dogs I've known have been obedient, but were hardly dispirited. If a man enjoys seeing a dog run free with no regard for his master, then there are several breeds to be recommended to him, none of which are bird dogs. There is a non-mysterious combination of discipline and love that will turn any puppy into an obedient—but not spiritless—bird dog.

In a greatly simplified definition lifted from the guidebook of the Mulak Institute of Corrective Dog Behavior, dog training amounts to a demonstration phase in which the dog is shown what you want of him, followed by an enforcement phase consisting of repetition in a controlled situation with rewards for performance and reprimands for improper behavior. This is true of all dog training, no matter what is being taught.

The enforcement part involves reward when the dog does *right*. Every puppy has his own "handle"—the one thing that he best responds to. Some will do anything for a treat, some love to fetch things. With others, praise is everything they'll ever want. Dog trainers will tell you to find your pup's handle, then use it and use it and use it.

No problem there.

But the other half of the equation calls for reprimand when the dog does wrong. In my part of the country, humane people have done a wonderful job in many areas that needed their good attentions. Some, however, have taken the idea of "humane treatment" too far and have produced an almost McCarthyish fear among folks. People act as though there isn't much you can do to a dog this side of raising your voice, and they're not too sure about that.

Like Frank Roach, who I quoted in the opening epigram, I wish I could just leave the dog a note. I really do. But that won't work. You need to be physical. Get mad, jump up and down, or swat him with your hat if you have to—but *physically* let him know that what he has done is the direct cause of your displeasure. If the dog wants to please you—and most dogs do—sometimes that's all it takes.

Grabbing dogs by their collars in this situation is something I don't like to do for several reasons, but mostly because the dogs I've owned have usually been smaller than me, and there seems to be a leverage effect that can damage their necks. Another reason has to do with the number of times I must collar them when I'm *not* reprimanding them.

Instead, when it becomes necessary to get physical, I grab a handful of ear and face and lead them to the scene of the crime. They don't like it, and tend to remember what it is I'm angry about. (In regard to using ears as handles, I should say that if you yank hard enough you can injure your dog—but I think you realize that. Lyndon Johnson got himself into a heap of trouble when he lifted his basset hound by the ears a few years back, so I'd advise against doing this sort of thing on national TV if you're the president of a large country.)

A rhetorical question: Why is it that just about every dog will sit on command, but there isn't one in a dozen that will stop when his owner hollers "Whoa!"? The "whoa" command is certainly the more useful and important of the two. The difference, of course, is in the enforcement.

This is where the gladiators are separated from the gladiolas. To enforce "sit" the trainer gently pushes on the dog's rear end until he sits. It's easy, and it gets results. Enforcement of "whoa," however, does not involve gently doing anything. Instead, you must chase after the dog and physically pick him up and return him to the spot where he was supposed to stop, and do it all in a way that lets Sparky know you are unhappy with his performance. It has to be done that way. *Asking* him to stop won't work. Neither will chewing him out, arguing with him, or telling him what you're going to do if he doesn't get with the program. There are times when nothing short of smacking the dog will suffice. At such times, don't fool around— smack him. It has nothing to do with your being a nice guy or an SOB. It has a great deal to do with your being an effective trainer.

Universally, the people who have success training dogs realize that dogs are *animals*, and that they are *animal trainers*. Human kindness is fine, but only when applied to humans. Each day, you should have a chitchat with your dog. It should begin with, "You, Sparky, are a dog. That means you are an animal, not a person. Do you understand that?" Then (and this is the most important part of the whole chitchat) "Do I?"

3. I can't hear you over the static.

Whoa...I said whoa. Now stop...Hey, I said hold it!...You, whoa! Right now!...Did you hear me? I said whoa, dammit...WHOA!...Don't take another step or I'm gonna swatcha one...Now stay right there...Hey, who told you to move? Did I say go ahead?...Hold it!...You stop when I say whoa...Dammit, come back here. Whoa!

Don't blame Sparky—hell, you'd run away too. Unfortunately, that tirade is not an exaggeration. Both you and I have heard far worse.

Dog handlers are supposed to put out information, and bird dogs are supposed to pick it up. But let's face it, even a smart dog is not highly conversant in the English language.

Anything the dog cannot understand is static and, in essence, bad information. By their actions, dogs have been trying to teach us that for a long time. A certain amount of muttering is forgivable, but dog handlers—the good ones—are careful to use clear, consistent commands that the dog is capable of picking up. The best check is to just listen to yourself once in a while—use a pocket tape recorder if you have one, but listen. How many times do you repeat a command? How much static do you put out? How many words? How many *syllables?*

After twenty years in the engine room of a ship, my hearing is not what it once was. I seem to hear my wife better when she prefaces her conversations with my name, as in "Steven, the TV is too loud." It works with dogs, too. Whenever I use the dog's name first, the chances that he will hear my command and do what I'm asking are improved considerably.

My brother once had a dog that he named Dusty, and when we hunted together with my dog Duffy, it proved to be a most graphic illustration of the canine version of the old "sounds like" game. I resolved to be careful of that sort of thing whenever I could. And it doesn't just involve names, either. "Whoa" always sounded like "No" to me. When George Bird Evans made an issue out of substituting the nonconfusing word "Hold" in place of "Whoa," I jumped to it. I've been shouting "Hut!" to five generations of dogs since.

I have walked behind men at field trials who only spoke to their dogs when they were doing wrong. When you listen to yourself talking to your dog, be sure that each rebuke for a wrong is balanced with praise for something done right. Both represent useful information. And while there is much to be conveyed by the tone of your voice, there is seldom any positive information in that.

Be aware that your dog is hungry for information. It can take the form of the spoken word, a whistle, a hand signal, or even the signs you give him through body language. Be sure the signals you send him are in a form he can understand.

4. Your lips tell me no, but it's yes in your heart.

Dogs are not robots with an on/off switch. The dog is learning whenever he is with you—not just during actual training sessions. Since you can't stop Sparky from learning, it follows that whatever you *permit* the dog to do (that is, whatever goes uncorrected), you are *teaching* the dog to do. If you are permitting him to sit on the car seat, then you are *teaching* him to sit on the car seat. If you let him chew on the birds he's retrieving, then you are *teaching* him to chew on birds. Piddling in the cellar, jumping on people's laps, barking—anything: If you're there, *you're teaching him to do it.*

Based on that, one might argue—and people like me often do—that a puppy should not be allowed to do anything that he will later have to be taught *not* to do. That goes for domestic things as well as chasing birds and running amuck in the field. Believe me, compared to *un*training, not permitting bad habits to take hold is a piece of cake.

This is a terrible thing to say—the sort that a sensible man would deny if he were quoted—but training a dog can be a good way to find out if you've got the temperament to raise kids. It takes commitment. Your dog will be as good as you want him to be. Again: The currency in dog training is *time*, and you can find out just how good you want him to be by figuring out how much of that currency you're willing to spend on him.

There are no secrets to dog training, but if there were, one of them would be that anyone can have a good dog just so long as he or she adheres to the "steady strain" approach to dog training; five or ten minutes per day *every day* is a steady strain, and gets far better results than an hour once a week on a Saturday. Good dogs require an investment in long-term training.

And remember that you're training him even when you don't think you are.

5. I don't have to obey you unless...

This lesson should be news to nobody. It says that inconsistency of enforcement—that is, allowing Sparky to decide which commands he wants to obey—is a mistake.

Effective training is a matter of controlling the situation. Circumstances where you do not have some measure of control should be avoided. When you're starting out, it's a good idea to keep a check cord on your puppy—that's control. Conduct your first few lessons in a fenced-in yard where distractions are at a minimum. That's control, too.

Ultimately you have to do some training afield, and "controlling the situation" amounts to your own physical enforcement of your commands. So it follows that if you holler "whoa" but Sparky decides to keep running, you should be in a position to do something about it. It might mean tugging on a check cord or pushing the zap button for a shock collar, but most of the time it means running after him and demonstrating your displeasure in an emphatic manner. Now, here's the rub: if you are not prepared to do that, then don't tell him to stop!

Sparky may be a dog, but he's no dummy. Every moment that he's with you he's learning and absorbing his training, both the positive and the negative. It doesn't take him long to figure out what he can get away with. And what he tries to teach you about your inconsistency is that "I don't have to obey the guy unless...":

a. He is within grabbing distance of me.
b. He tells me three times.
c. We are in the back yard.
d. He yells.
e. He puts a check cord on me.

Don't give him the chance to arrive at those conclusions. Be consistent.

If you're going to minimize frustration and enjoy your dog all through his lifetime, the most important lesson you can ever teach him is that he will receive immediate retribution whenever he does not do something you tell him to do. Don't think that you'll be constantly smacking your dog; once he learns The Big One you may never have to smack him again. You will have a trained dog. It's all a matter of consistency.

6. Look, Ma! No brakes!

I mentioned earlier that there wasn't one dog in a dozen that would stop on his owner's command. I was being charitable. Maybe it's more like one in fifty. "Whoa" (or a substitute such as "hold") is the most important command for any hunting dog, and the lack of that command is the primary reason there are so few good hunting dogs.

I could start now and end next Sunday listing reasons why a bird dog must be 100 percent reliable on the "whoa" command. I could, but I won't. It's enough to say that without it you have no control over the dog in the field, and without control you can teach nothing.

Here's a list of what I consider to be the five most important commands that you can teach to a bird dog:

1. "Whoa"
2. "Whoa"
3. "Whoa"
4. "Whoa"
5. "Whoa"

I don't mean to diminish any other aspect of dog training. Obedience training is certainly important. By the time he's three years old, a well-trained bird dogs will know thirty words and at least as many physical signals of one sort or another. Although there are enough books on obedience training to occupy several shelves at the local library, whenever I'm asked, I recommend Richard A. Wolters' *Gun Dog*.

But, again, if you can teach "whoa" to your hunting dog, you don't have much else to worry about.

7. How far is too far?

"The trouble with most bird dogs is a matter of range. Funny, though, I've never met a man whose dog was half-way obedient who had a problem with range." My friend Tom Lamica strung those two sentences together years ago. Tommy made a small living out of turning untrained dogs into hunters. He did it mostly with obedience, which says a lot about problem solving as it applies to bird dogs.

Chief among his bag of tricks was the command, "Out front!" Accompanied by a hand signal, it required the dog to get in front of the handler. Once Tom had the dog trying to stay in front of him, he could teach the dog to cast back and forth by shifting directions as he walked, calling the dog to the front at each reverse of direction.

Using the same method, he was also able to control the dog's range. When the dog started to get too far out, Tom would turn around and yell, "Out front!" I've used it on my dogs, and the dogs that I train, and all of them have learned very quickly what "Out front!" means. It keeps the dogs where they belong, and teaches them the habit of checking in, which isn't such a bad idea either.

Ultimately, the invisible leash works best at controlling the dog's range. There are always times—usually during the first twenty minutes or so—when Sparky decides he knows more about range than you or I. At such times, there is no substitute for running after your dog and clearly letting him know that you mean business. After that, "Out front!" is usually all it takes.

8. Attention, please!

I made the point earlier that successful training de-pends on being able to control the situation. Training with a buddy who's only along to keep you company dimin-ishes that level of control because it distracts both you and Sparky. If your buddy is a professional bird dog trainer—a

Frank Roach or a Richard Wolters—then by all means bring him with you. Most likely, he'll know enough not to distract you or the dog. Or if your buddy is willing to actually help—work a check cord or plant pigeons—welcome him as well. The bottom line is that when a dog is on the ground during a training session, he needs—and deserves—*all* of your attention. Usually, your friend's presence only adds to the dog's confusion.

Training with another dog around is nearly always a mistake. Sparky is not going to learn anything from the dog. Nothing useful, that is. Dogs have a tendency to react to one another in a way that is universally counter-productive to training. Your attention as a trainer is split, even if the other dog is "fully trained." You can't win at that game. So don't play it.

Hunting season, on the other hand, is *not* training time. It is the time to enjoy the fruits of your labors. If your buddy wants to go with you then, fine. And if he wants to bring his dog, that's okay too.

But training is best done alone.

9. Birds, birds, birds!

After a lecture on dog training, I spoke to a man who was enthusiastic about getting started with his Brittany puppy. "I'm going to begin the first thing tomorrow," he told me. "Me and Sparky are headed up to Swift River."

"Why there?" I asked. Swift River was the local wildlife management area.

"Hell, that's where the pheasants are."

I shouldn't have been disappointed, but I was. My talk had been entitled "The Invisible Leash of Obedience," and if I had mentioned game birds, I wasn't aware of it.

The idea behind this lesson is that birds are not necessary in the early training of a bird dog. Obedience and handling are much more important to the dog's early development. Before Sparky gets into birds, where you'll have very little control of the situation, he should have the invisible leash of obedience on him.

Here's a point I believe in enough to repeat: If a bird dog is nothing more than a life support system for a nose, then we don't teach the nose anything; the dog himself teaches his nose everything it will ever know. All the training we give to the dog is addressed to the life-support system.

And for that, you don't need birds.

10. Was it something I did?

"You know, I paid good money for this dog." The man had just been told by the judge (me) to pick up because his Brittany wouldn't stop on command and had run past another dog's point and flushed a planted pheasant. The man shook his head. "I've worked with him *for weeks.*"

"That's a good start," I told him. "Your dog's got all the desire in the world—keep at it."

But I knew he'd give up. When he wrote out the check for his puppy, he thought he had bought quality. Instead, he had bought potential. Then, walking out of the bird field with his dog on a lead, he didn't see quality as worth the additional cost he suddenly realized he must pay.

It is a sad commentary when a man who can afford thousands of dollars for guns and hunting rigs and the best in boots and clothes cannot seem to afford the time it takes to properly train a dog. People expect instant results, but dog training, like so many other worthwhile things in life, is far more a journey than a destination—a journey that too many dog owners give up on. Of all the bird dog training mistakes, "giving up" is probably the worst.

Like the man who scatters an expensive package of tomato seeds out of his window and then expects to harvest picture-perfect tomatoes, so, too, is the man who buys a well-bred puppy then takes him hunting and wonders why he "ain't like the picture on the package." You have to start them correctly, tend them with care, harden them off, set them in at the right time, nurture them with the things they need, support them as they grow, and be wise enough to enjoy the fruit they produce, regardless of whether or not it looks exactly like the picture on the package.

Those are the top ten "lessons" our dogs have been trying to teach us. The fact that we repeat them so often means we're not learning from our mistakes. You may have recognized a few that you've made. However, it's never too late. You can always turn that mistake into a lesson; recognizing it is a good place to start.

It was Amy's second season, so this was a few years back. We were on our way out of Compass covert. We had seen some birds—Amy even pointed one—but there was nothing in my game bag except a few empty shells. The way back to the road took us across a muddy brook recently bridged by a deadfall. The tree trunk was just a few inches in diameter, so I found a long stick to use as a walking staff and crossed to the other side.

Let me say, before going on, that the only command I never had to tell Amy twice was "Go ahead"—she was an expert at "Go ahead" from the very beginning. From the start she always hunted like her fur was on fire. But this time she was afraid of the tightrope act and stayed behind. I cajoled and commanded her, I even said "Go ahead" a few times, but she would not cross the brook. My thoughts ran along the lines of "I'll be damned if I'm going over and carrying her across; let her swim if she's so afraid of getting up on the log."

I started off, figuring desperation would bring her across, but all Amy did was run back and forth on the far side, crying and complaining. She seem determined not to cross. It was pitiful.

Finally I went back, balanced across, lifted her, and placed her on the deadfall bridge. The "demonstration phase" worked: she scampered to the other side. Then, like a kid that finally learns to ride a bike after being afraid, she wouldn't stop. She ran back, and then across again. If she could talk, she would have been saying, "Hey, this is a piece of cake!"

"Well, that's fine," I said. "Now get off the log and go sit down while I cross." She ran to the other side and waited for me.

It was like something from *Ripley's Believe It or Not*. I was no sooner on the deadfall when the dog decided to give me one last exhibition of just how easy all this was. Little John and Robin Hood had nothing on us. Of course, I was Robin Hood, and Little John taught me a "lesson."

After she tripped me and I was standing waist-deep in the muddy water, that all-white dog made the mistake of remaining on the deadfall where I could lunge and reach her.

So I played out the part of the blind man in the joke whose seeing-eye dog peed on his pants leg. He reached out his hand, saying, "Good boy, good boy."

"Why are you being nice to him?" someone asked. "Don't you know he just peed on your leg?"

"Oh, I know." replied the blind man. "I just want to find out where his head is so I can kick him in the butt."

The latter was a great grandson of Champion Graphic, although no one seemed especially interested in that fact.

W. H. Foster

two

The Components
of Greatness

Rusty approached the stand of aspens running boldly into the breeze. A big setter, he held his head high and seemed the very embodiment of style. But it appeared to the judge that Rusty had been working independently of his handler. The judge requested that the dog be turned and headed in the other direction.

Colonel Paul, who was Rusty's owner, gave the judge, who was me, a look that could chill a keg of warm beer. "Can't you see he's working a bird?"

This was a woodcock trial. All the dogs that I had ever seen (including my own) worked woodcock slowly and methodically. Rusty, I was to discover, was different.

If a bird dog's point can be defined as a dog halted while in action, then Colonel Paul's setter was that definition raised exponentially. Running, he was so graceful that he seemed a point put into motion. Thus, a few seconds later when he stopped, it took me a moment to realize he was pointing.

I may be dense, but I try not to make the same mistake twice in the same day. I kept my mouth shut. Colonel Paul walked in front of his dog-become-statue, and when a woodcock flushed a shot was fired with a blank pistol. Rusty had all four legs on the ground when he pointed, but at the sound of the shot one of them lifted. The Colonel barely glanced at his dog. The foot was replaced. Obviously the Colonel's nastiest looks were reserved for inexperienced judges. We walked away, leaving the dog on point.

"So you want to see him handle?" he said. I don't recall if there was any sarcasm in the Colonel's voice, but there should have been. "Rusty—let's go." he said. At that, the dog was immediately in front of us. Moments later, without a word to the dog, we made a ninety-degree turn. Rusty adjusted, continuing his windshield wiper imitation sixty yards in front of us. We made another arbitrary right turn, with a similar response from Rusty.

Somehow I had expected shouts, whistles, and hand signals, and didn't quite know how to react to a dog that didn't need any of that. Handling, I was to discover, is necessary only on a dog that *requires* handling. Rusty's problem had to do with the fact that he didn't need to be told what to do. I've made a study of problems, and not having to tell the dog what to do is a good problem to have.

What is it that makes a superior bird dog like Rusty? If the best dogs I had seen up to that point were Cadillacs, then Rusty was a Rolls Royce. Why? Or, more pragmatically, how?

A dog breeder will tell you it is bloodlines: good dogs selectively bred to other good dogs, with careful attention paid to the results. And he would be right.

Another man, a professional trainer, will make a convincing case for a thoughtful training program methodically applied. And he'd be equally correct.

A third man, a hunter who works with his dog and sees him getting better year after year, might say experience is the key—lots and lots of birds. And he would be no less right than the previous two.

With Rusty, as with every other bird dog that has approached greatness, the correct answer to this multiple-choice exam is, "D: All of the above." Each of the three components is important, and, more than balance, there must be a harmony to the mix of ingredients. It isn't black magic or some erudite science— Colonel Paul, Rusty's owner/breeder/trainer, would be the first to tell you that. But you have to pay attention and put in some effort. And have a bit of luck.

Did Rusty win the woodcock trial, you ask? Is the pope Catholic?

Bill Puza was already an old man when I met him. He was a dog breeder from Westfield, and he started the Tekoa Mountain line of English setters. I suspect that if you were to walk by the place where he is buried, you might hear him rolling over in his grave because of what has been done to the line he started, but that's a subject for a different story.

Paramount among the unexplainable aspects of his life was that he liked me. I don't know why; as a young man, intensity and a definite lack of tact made up a large part of my personality. Oh, I played at training bird dogs, but even though I was seldom right, I was never in doubt. Hell, back then I was so hardheaded that even *I* had trouble liking me. Nevertheless, Bill took a shine to me. For my part, with the exception of a brief three-minute period, I loved the man like a father for as long as he lived.

My first setter, Hazel, was a line-bred product of a Bill Puza Tekoa Mountain breeding. On a spring day in 1980 she pointed three pheasants in front of 150 mostly dog club folks who, if not actually gentlemen, were dressed as if they were. Hazel had wrapped up the derby stake before we left the bird field. I was basking in my own moment of glory as a dog trainer when I happened to overhear Bill Puza acknowledge someone's compliment. He was talking about Hazel. What he said contained the phrase, "Yep, I breed some good ones."

Need I say more about the three minutes?

The things the dog inherits from his parents—his breeding—make up the most traceable component of greatness. There are a countless number of traits involved in bloodlines, everything from coloration and size to highly visible performance factors like staunchness and style on point.

Those are all matters of potential. A Stradivarius might be capable of all the nuances of Tchaikovsky's impossible concerto, but it is only potential until a fiddler runs a bow across the strings. A well-bred dog might be capable of becoming one of the great ones, but how do you get the music to play?

Among the many bloodline traits, and overshadowing them all in importance, is *trainability*. It is a measure of the dog's receptiveness to things taught *by* people, and his willingness to work *for* people. Some dogs train easily and stay trained. Others seem to forget as fast as they're taught. When a trainer can begin with a dog that has a high degree of trainability, all the other things in a bird dog's potential can be brought out. Without it, a bird dog's life can become an endless series of refresher courses in remedial field work and obedience.

It is often difficult to see through the results of training—or, in other cases, the results of a lack of training—and discover the basic quality of the dog that lies beneath it all. Well-trained, obedient dogs are a pleasure to hunt with; they regularly win field trials, seldom bite their owners, and are generally "nice people." If you're looking to breed your bird dog, they say that's the kind you should seek out. But be careful. As with so many other things, *they* don't always know what *they're* talking about. Trainability is in the blood. Training is not. Manners tends to reflect the quality of the trainer rather than that of the dog.

Breeders deserve all of the credit for the natural ability contained in every bird dog. No dog that is a "pointing fool" got there by accident. And the truly great ones have potential to spare.

It wasn't the puppy's first point, but it was as close to entirely voluntary as anything yet. I had kicked up the woodcock and she had stood still. I was smiling. She had now pointed one in a row, which, considering her past performance, was pretty good.

She started working scent again; her tail traced rapid circles in the air and her nose was nearly in the dead leaves and bloodroot flowers. I stood on her check cord to stop her, then lifted her head so that her nose was scenting the air. I've watched as woodcock walk in a seemingly aimless series of circles, hairpins, and figure-eights as they feed. The scent pattern they put down has to resemble a maze. It must be a natural defense against predators that hunt with their noses. A trailing dog will have problems with the maze, but a dog that seeks out body scent can go directly to the bird.

A moment later the puppy had her head back down. My old Winnie was a woodcock dog of the first degree, but even she loved to put her nose down and smell those footprints once in a while. I stepped on the check cord of Winnie's replacement once again. When this one gets to be as good as Winnie was, maybe I'll occasionally look the other way. But today she needed to learn the right technique. Still, as I lifted the pup's head, I found that I was using the same gentle touch I needed in training that other woodcock dog a dozen years before.

"A bird dog is little more than a life-support system for a nose." That's a description my hunting partner likes to sight when we argue about things doggie. His definition becomes relevant when you stop to consider that just about everything that man teaches dog is directed at the life-support-system part. Man teaches only the dog, not the nose: range and casting, retrieving, obedience, yard and field manners—all of these could just as easily be taught to a dog without any nose at all; it would make little difference.

So does that mean training isn't important? Nothing could be further from the truth. Training is imperative.

No matter how much potential there is in the Stradivarius, unless the fiddler is trained and the instrument tuned, the music will never play. The training Sparky gets as a puppy will define the margins within which he can develop. Inside those margins, Sparky can learn to hunt and fulfill his potential. Without them he is destined to be as bad a dog as his owner is willing to put up with.

It begins with basics. I've written plenty of stories about hunting and dog work in the field, but never one about yard training. I suspect the reason has little to do with importance or reality, but lies more with the definition of what's fun and what's work.

A well-trained field dog, when seen from the outside, is very impressive. Helping a bird dog learn to hunt is easy, since the dog wants to hunt in the first place. I didn't mean "easy" as in "no effort." I meant easy compared to training an animal to do something he doesn't want to do; there are people, after all, who train horses to run around with a man on their back or tigers to jump through flaming rings while not eating anyone.

Some people think of a "good dog" as one that is the product of a training method that makes them little more than instruments of the hunter's will, hunting machines with no initiatives of their own. That's okay for seeing-eye dogs, but who wants to *hunt* with a dog like that? On a pheasant shooting trip to Texas a few years back I had an opportunity to observe some Labrador retrievers that pretty much met that "machine" definition. Each was some sort of champion. They were near perfection on re-trieves—just so long as the gunner had held up his end of the bargain and killed the bird dead. Where the dogs came up short was on down-but-not-out pheasants. Those dogs were such an extension of their handler's will that they didn't have the wherewithal to track down a running cripple. The handler had no command for "be dogs," so they remained robots. We lost a bunch of birds. Overtraining had turned good dogs into joyless automatons.

Hazel didn't bother with the open area, but instead raced along the lee side of the thorns and tangles that choked the cow path. I glanced back at the old barn and farmhouse, now well behind us, and calculated that we had traveled a distance of roughly one pheasant-flight. Just as I did, the dog seconded the motion: she slowed as she digested the signals on the breeze. There was a moment when she seemed to lose the scent, but after some running and backtracking she pointed for an instant, then went soft and moved ahead again. Nonhunters think the only way a bird dog tells you something is by pointing, but

Hazel's message said a great deal about the artful dodger who was trying to hide from us. She had another quivering point that quickly melted. My setter started ahead, then, with a third time finality, stopped in an abrupt freeze-frame, looking hard into a juniper.

I circled to get in front of her, and a moment later the pheasant came clattering into the air, cackling obscenities and spewing a white stream behind it. The gun came up easily and the rooster fell—a few moments later I knelt to take the bird as Hazel brought it in.

It was an impressive piece of work. In her fifth season, Hazel had mastered a hunting method that searched the most probable places first. She no longer spent time delving into thick cover, but instead allowed the wind to bring her the story of what was going on beyond. And she not only found birds, she handled them. Most charming of all, I didn't have anything to do with her figuring it out.

What differentiates a bird dog from other types is *not* their ability to find a bird—any mongrel that breathes through his nose can do that. No, it's *how* Sparky goes about it and what he does with the bird *after* he finds it that defines a bird dog. More than just finding, what you and I expect from a bird dog is an effective search method that we call *hunting*. (To avoid confusion, my own term for what the dog does is "hunt/search.") Then we want him to *handle* the bird in a manner that will present us with a chance to shoot it on our terms. That handling process is defined as *bird sense.*

Neither hunt/search nor bird sense are things that are bred into a dog; they only come about through training—not through training that you or I give Sparky, but through that which he gives himself. It amounts to experience.

Of the three components of greatness, experience is the most elusive. Men, after all, are in control of Sparky's bloodlines, and certainly are responsible for his training, but we are little more than observers—fans, maybe—as the dog goes about teaching himself what he needs to know about hunting and bird sense. Semantically, experience differs from training and education. I didn't teach Hazel that business about searching the most productive cover first—just the opposite. There was a time when I tried to get her to cast back and forth mechanically. And it wasn't me who taught her to let the wind bring her news of the birds' whereabouts. Hell, that was my voice you used to hear yelling, "Get in there and find that bird!"

Man trains the dog, but when it comes to educating the nose part, Sparky teaches himself. We can encourage him. We establish a goal and the boundaries, but the dog needs to find the goal by himself if it's to be worthwhile. We enforce the boundaries, and keep him on the playing field. We can reward him when he's done a good job, and let him know we're unhappy about the rabbit he decided to point. But mostly the dog is pretty much on his own.

My dad used to say that you had to take your dog out before the season to give him a chance to "sharpen-up his nose." Maybe so. It's Sparky's own success and failures—and his ability to learn from them—that show him the correct way. Education, after all, is knowledge digested. How many successes and failures—how many birds—will it take before the dog becomes wise? Experience tends to stick to those who are willing to pay attention to it. That means a good dog is a quick learner. But the short answer to that question is, "As many as it takes." The best you can do is take him out as much as possible so he can get a lot of those successes and failures.

So we return to our rhetorical question: Just how did Rusty arrive at that degree of excellence that so few others ever approach? How do you make a superior bird dog? I've always been suspicious of folks who answer a question with a question, but the answers in this case really are more questions: How smart is the dog? Does he have it in him? How predisposed is he to learn from his own experiences? How important is it that he make you happy?

And (here's a real kicker) how important is it for you to find out how good he might be?

Every detail of what makes a good bird dog may be figured out someday, but don't bet on it. It's been twenty years since I first saw Rusty, but I still don't have a good answer to that question of "how?" Neither does Colonel Paul, nor anyone else I know. We work with bird dogs, trying to get the best out of them. Every once in a while—once in a lifetime, maybe—a truly superb dog results.

The great ones, including Rusty, seem to train themselves. That's because they are trainable. They learn from their experiences and often seem to have a lifetime of bird sense after just a couple of seasons. Their owners, if they are wise, worry about them dying young.

To be sure, there is more art than science involved in dog training. There is a house-that-Jack-built relationship among the building blocks of a great bird dog. In chapter eight, I address the idea of timing as it pertains to those relationships. What can be said for sure is that without a blend of the three components—breeding, training, and experience—the music never plays.

A mere man wouldn't know, for all he smells is the September night.

Aldo Leopold
Red Lanterns

three

The Pointing
Addiction

I guess we're addicts.

Like all addicts, we don't really comprehend the thing
we're addicted to. A new owner shows off his puppy's
pointing ability while we watch. A wing dangled from a
fishing rod is the standard game. The pup chases, and
after a few minutes he realizes that he's not going to
outrun the wing. The pup strikes a pointing pose as he
crouches to make a jump. In that moment, his proud
owner smiles and says, "He's going to be a good one—did
you see him point?"

Did we see him? Hell, we could look at nothing else!

I love it, this addiction of ours, but I can't understand it. Somewhere in between that first puppy-crouch and the awkward-but-beautiful point of a mature bird dog something happens that I don't fully grasp.

Oh, I have the basics down: The dog scents the bird but arrests his instinct to pounce; the point is the result of immobility caused by the tension of the opposing forces. But as with so many other phenomena, I'm left far behind when I try to follow an elementary idea as it becomes an elegant process—a process that actually finds birds when they are trying hard not to be found. When I was back in school I got pretty good marks in science, and I was employed for twenty years as a marine engineer, so I want you to know that admitting I cannot comprehend a scientific principal doesn't come easy.

But any technology, when sufficiently advanced, soon becomes indistinguishable from magic. You and I can understand how a tuning fork vibrates and creates the sonic waves that we hear as sound. Yes, sound is vibration. But where I get lost is when that same principle is raised by several levels of complexity. When, for example, sound is applied to an optical disk and read by a machine that can recreate every nuance of a Chopin concerto or the tremble in Emmylou Harris's voice.

That's not physics—that's a minor miracle.

The music plays, a dog points a hiding grouse, and we stand in awe. We *know* it happens. That's obvious. But trying to understand the process gives us brain cramps. Addiction, on the other hand, is easy. It only takes appreciation.

My old Brittany stopped in midstride, his nostrils flared. Stretching ever higher, he turned to the left, finally rising up on his hind legs, much as he would at home when he "danced" for a dog biscuit. His message had a lucidity about it: Something that only his nose detected drifted in the air just over his head. He started up the hillside in me-

thodical pursuit of the fleeing scent. I understood my role. I followed.

Sixty yards farther along, on the far side of the ridge, he pointed before a tumbledown stone fence. I circled widely, then paraded along both sides of the old wall with my gun at port arms. No bird flushed. I waved Duff ahead but, of course, he wouldn't move. Exasperated, I finally got down on my hands and knees and examined the face of the wall where he was pointing. Immediately under the dog's nose one of the stones turned into a grouse, sitting with its head pulled into its breast feathers, dying from my "missed" shot that had put two pellets into its belly half an hour before.

My shooting hadn't gotten that bird—Duffy's nose had. Yet he sat aloof, wearing his Charles de Gaulle ho-hum look. (That was Duffy in his last season, when it seemed nothing could excite him anymore. He was cool.) As I've so often done before, I lifted the grouse to my own nose and smelled—nothing at all.

How do dogs do it? Every day of his life Duffy continually amazed me—not because he was exceptional, but because he wasn't. Duffy and every other dog has an ability in his nose that amazes and fascinates me. Think of it. You return home from visiting friends who own a dog. Your dogs feast upon your pantlegs with their noses, breathing in a banquet of something you have no way of knowing is there. What are they sniffing?

When I brought my New England grouse dogs to Texas for the first time, they hunted birds they'd never seen before. Admittedly, they had more than enough trouble with ground cactus, but they pointed both blue quail and bobwhites on first encounter, while ignoring roadrunners and other ground birds they'd not known previously. What is it about scent that allows bird dogs to recognize game birds they've never even been told about?

Or how about this one: Last fall I hunted along a wooded margin where the smell of freshly spread rotted manure from an adjoining pasture was overpowering. My setter worked and pointed a half-dozen woodcock, apparently indifferent to the odor that nearly gagged me. The incomprehensible things that dogs regularly do with their noses! The list could go on.

We humans tend to measure everything in terms of our five limited and imperfect senses, yet things such as radio waves and ultraviolet light exist all around us. We need instruments to prove it, but in this half of the twentieth century, no one other than my Uncle Walter disbelieves their existence. The rest of nature does not operate under the limitations of our five human senses. Consider the radar of bats, or the "extended feel" of the lateral lines of fish, or the common will of colony insects, or the homing instincts of migratory birds—all observed phenomena, the explanations for which are mostly theory.

Similarly, there's a theory that can still be found in *bad* books about dogs. It contends that the scenting ability of bird dogs (and other predatory animals) is simply an improved version of the sense of smell as we know it. Some opinions claim that a dog's sense of smell is hundreds of times more powerful than our own.

Don't believe it.

Scenting is not smelling. Duffy didn't find that dying grouse by smelling it. A dog has something in his nose that you and I can hardly imagine, and to say that it's just a high-performance smeller is like saying that a bird's wing and a human hand are pretty much the same thing since the bone structure is similar. To be sure, a dog uses his nose to gather scent, so scenting is probably an evolved form of a sense of smell. But when all the special abilities of a dog's nose are considered, the evidence points to a unique ability for which humans have no equivalent.

If you're waiting for a scientific explanation of scent, take note that the scientists are still puzzled by the phenomenon of olfactory fatigue in our *own* noses. (Olfactory fatigue is the reason the monkey house at the zoo smells like a monkey house when you first walk in, then after a few minutes you don't notice it anymore.) They've come up with machines that can measure nearly anything, including odors, yet animal scent remains a mystery.

A mystery to science, that is. Not to dogs.

Dogs might be defined as instruments for measuring and detecting scent. Reading that meter takes some education on our part, and the first lesson is that dogs don't lie. They might act like a meter out of calibration—or nonselective, or overly sensitive, or even just plain wrong—but they don't lie. If Sparky says there is scent here, believe him.

"It makes you wonder," is a common expression. Surely it must have first been uttered by a dog owner. "What did he scent that made him turn abruptly?" "How could he walk by that downed bird without seeing it?" Or my favorite, "Why is he rolling in that?" It makes you wonder.

I said as much to my friend Frank Roach one time. A pointer of his was rolling in a Texas cow flop. What I said was something along the lines of, "For a few minutes I'd like to be a dog, just so I could understand why they do that."

Frank can hardly be described as jovial, but he laughed at his own semi-profound reply: "Steve," he said. "If you were ever a dog for five minutes, I think we'd have a hell of a time ever getting you to come back."

The more I know about dogs and the more I wonder about scenting, the more certain I am that he was right.

When we started off again, Hazel slashed through the cover behind the barn, unaware that the grouse was near. She was accelerating out of a turn when the scent hit her, and the beautiful clumsiness of her skidding point resembled the unfolding of an uncooperative lawn chair. In that instant she had the bird pinned. It was the sort of thing I wait all year to see, and I was still smiling when the bird went up. The shot was quick and clean, and Hazel almost danced as she made the retrieve. It's a glorious occasion each time I take a grouse, but Hazel's point made this one extra special.

What goes on when a dog scents a bird?

Much of the charm of that question lies in the fact that no one seems to know for sure. When the dogs of people's imaginations have ethereal qualities, it always has to do with their ability to discover things by scent. There are, however, a few things we can say with some certainty: Dogs' noses vary in ability; temperature and humidity have an effect on performance; and if a dog works into the wind his chances of finding a bird are improved. But even those pieces of information are based on observation rather than on any objective measurement.

Let's face it, we can smell but we can't scent. Outside of a farmer finding his way to the hen house in the dark, there aren't too many men who regularly find birds by using their sense of smell. Yet the absolute worst bird dog that ever wagged a tail has an ability that defies explanation.

There is a huge body of evidence which indicates that a dog lives in a world where his primary sense organ is not his eyes, but his nose. That's why he always keeps it pointed where he's going. It is something that we as visual beings find all but impossible to fathom. Vision is about as important to a dog as hearing is to us. In the field, a dog uses his sight to keep from bumping into things and his ears to keep track of his master. Everything else—from locating the birds he's hunting to finding a brook to drink from—he does with his nose.

Through his nose he comprehends his world.

What about the dog that seemed to be following pheasant tracks in the snow? He made a wrong turn and lost the scent trail even though you were right behind him and could plainly see that the bird's tracks went in the other direction. *Sparky, can't you see!*

Or the classic case that I seem to witness at least once every hunting season: an air-washed bird falls stone dead and in plain sight, yet, looking only with his nose, the dog can't find the bird until he literally steps on it. Sparky *won't* see. A dog's eyes report only movement. An unmoving object with no odor goes unnoticed.

Sometimes, when one dog scents a bird and his bracemate does not, I wonder if a dog's nose is like a TV: there's nothing wrong with the bracemate's scenting ability, his TV was just tuned to a different channel at the time.

She made her turn at the field margin and was accelerating when she struck it. Her body spun around as she fought to stop against her forward momentum. The scent hung just above the frost. Mixed in with the poultry smell of feathers and the odor of dust and feces was the dark liquid scent of fear, and she sorted through the mixed multitude of signals in her nostrils to read that and that alone. She moved two steps closer, then a third before she sensed that the bird was in limbo— trapped just enough so that it wouldn't run, yet not frightened enough to fly.

My hunting partner explained that his wirehair would follow a scent trail until she came to an obstacle—a brush pile or a deadfall or a stone fence—anything that would keep the dog from continuing on, but through which the bird could keep going. Rather 'han leave the scent trail and pick it up again on the other side, the dog would go on point. Only when her handler would go to her and signal her ahead would she move on.

It seemed obvious that the dog wasn't so much pointing as waiting, like a piece of equipment going into reset
when faced with something it wasn't programmed to
handle. If you take that as an explanation of what the dog
is doing, a better picture emerges as to what's going on in
a bird dog's nose.

I had a Brittany whose scenting abilities were either
better or worse than the wirehair's. She followed scent, but
would go into that reset-type point whenever there was
any variation in the trail. She was a notorious "false
pointer." Other dogs, whose noses have a still different
degree of sensitivity and accuracy, seem able to literally
run down the scent trail and arrive at a place in space and
time where the bird is just ahead of them, and only then
will they go on point. They bump a few, but their reset
adjustment is cranked all the way down.

*When Suzie saw that both men were returning, she
continued her search out into the stubble. The scent grew
stronger, but it was scattered on the breeze across the
open field. She worked the air, weaving back and
forth, but she could isolate none of the several
different scents being carried to her. Suddenly
she recalled a situation from years before.
She and her old kennelmate were hunting
stubble then, too. They had been unable to
unravel the unclear combination of scents
that became weaker when they tried to
follow them. There had been many pheasants
in the stubble that day, and those that had
run out escaped in the confusion of scents.*

*Remembering that, she realized there must be several
pheasants now running away from her toward the far
brush line. She circled to the right, urging her sore legs to
run. She turned back into the field when she reached the
brush along the edge. In the distance she saw her master
and the other man crossing toward her. The birds had to be
between them and her. The wind came over her tail, mov-*

ing the scent away from her as she cast through the rows, but she was certain the pheasants were here.

And how about the opposition? I've often wondered just how aware game birds are of the scent they leave behind them. Someone who has watched bird dogs for a while might conclude that there seems to be two types of scent given off by game birds—a lingering type that they put down by walking, and a more fleeting air-borne scent that comes from their bodies.

Just how aware of their own scent game birds are is subject to any number of interpretations. There is the they're-smarter-than-you-think school of thought. We hear, for example, of wise old rooster pheasants that double back on their own trails, and of grouse hopping into trees to confuse a following bird dog.

Smarts?

I'm not so sure. They may have more brains than a barnyard chicken, but it's hard to think of game birds as being in the rocket scientist category. But then, think of what a wild bird must face every day in order to survive: foxes, weasels, coyotes, bobcats— all *scenting* predators, all out to make a meal of him, and all of them doing it on a full-time basis. Admittedly, those wild predators must physically catch the bird rather than just get close and point it, but no matter what a bird dog's breeding or training, at best he is only a part-time hunter compared to a fox who does it to fill his belly.

If wild birds survive—and, of course, they do—it has to be by a combination of instincts rather than a conscious awareness of their scent trails. Grouse seem to have the brains of a burglar alarm—not smarts, really, just a pre-programmed set of specific reactions to specific stimuli. Pheasants run, trusting the infantry far more than the air force. Strongly scented woodcock trace patterns of loops and zigzags as they feed, leaving a scent maze to confuse any trailing predator. (That explains why the best woodcock dogs keep their heads high.) None of these birdy defense strategies is thought out, but rather, something game birds do instinctively. (Instinct, of course, makes for a wonderful explanation of just about any sort of animal behavior that we can't account for otherwise.)

If the dog is indeed a scent meter, then it sometimes seems that scent, particularly in the case of a running bird, resembles not so much a painted line but rather dribbles from a leaky paint bucket—a drip here, another few there, maybe a big space between the next dribble, then more drips... As Sparky develops bird sense, he learns to draw a conclusion from those drips and drabs, learning where to look for the next clue when the big spaces occur, assembling a conclusion from the series and acting upon it. An unsmart dog will search and trail and search and trail, and all his life never be able to do anything with a running bird except bust him up.

Sparky gets birdy for a minute or two, then continues on. Has a bird given him the slip, or was it just a false alarm? How many birds slip away that we, as nonscenting predators, never realize were there in the first place? Whenever I try to estimate the percentage of birds that evade even the best of dogs, no matter what number I care to use I always feel that it's too low.

Fear. The scent hit her as abruptly as if she had run into a wire fence. She knew she was too close to the bird and dared not move.

"Point!" Her master's voice carried faintly across the distance. She heard the men coming, but she couldn't shift even her eyes. In front of her something moved in the weeds. She didn't move.

The men drew closer, and the fear smell grew more intense. Then, the clatter of wings and the sound of voices: "Hen...! There's another...! And a third one...!" No shots were fired.

"Hold up, Dad. She's got a whole flock corralled—there's got to be a rooster in here somewhere."

She couldn't move. The scent in her nostrils was stronger than ever.

We shall go on to the end...we shall fight on the beaches, we shall fight on the landing grounds, we shall fight in the fields and in the streets, we shall fight in the hills; we shall never surrender.

Sir Winston Churchill

Teaching
Old Dogs
New Tricks

"Any bird dog can earn his keep on retrieving alone." Among hunters, you won't get many arguments against the validity of that sentiment. The worst bird dog that ever wagged a tail certainly has more ability to locate a hiding cripple than you and I and a dozen other fellows crawling around the covert on our hands and knees, peeking under every bush and deadfall.

The retrieves that bird dogs make on outdoor TV shows make for lovely pictures. Yet, to a dogless hunter, those same shows make retrieving dogs appear as nothing more than a frivolous luxury. After all, anyone can be his own retriever so long as the birds are centered and fall cleanly on open ground, as they always do on TV. In the real world no hunter is as consistent as he would like to be. Hunters make mistakes. Retrieving dogs correct them.

There is a game I play in the back yard with my dogs. It's fun and good training at the same time. The dogs are told to sit while I walk the far end of the yard, planting one pheasant wing and pretending to plant several others in various places. (The dogs don't seem to be clever enough to watch closely and see where I actually hide the wing.) Once done, I walk to a distant spot and call them to me, make them heel for a few steps, then tell them to "find dead." Some wonderful competition ensues: a high-speed search, followed by a bit of in-your-face bravado as the winner brings in the wing. I'm sure the wing smells of nothing more than dog spit after a while, but the main idea of the game is that each dog is using his nose competitively. Along the way, the game gives me a chance to enforce a dozen different field commands.

The same can be applied to hunting. When you drop a bird, put Sparky at heel and go immediately to where you marked the bird down. Make the dog sit for a few seconds; that should calm him down a notch or two. Then, with all the calm you can muster, say "dead bird" or whatever command you use. (In early training, this phase might be accomplished on a leash to give the dog the idea that he should, at least at the outset, search around you in a short radius for the scent.)

Because Sparky needs to be calm, *you* need to be calm. You might not realize it, but the dog is taking cues from you, and if you're excited, he figures there must be something to be excited about. Letting Sparky break point to make the retrieve gets him pumped up at the exact wrong time; he needs to be methodical about that retrieving business.

"Fetch" should be the all-encompassing command; fetch means "do the whole thing right." I've caught myself saying "No!" when the dog drops the wing she's retrieving. The command that accompanies the replacing of the wing in the dog's mouth should be "fetch."

Some bird dogs don't need to be taught. You throw a ball, Sparky chases it and brings it back to you. You can keep throwing the ball until your arm falls off and he'll keep running it back. It doesn't take the same dog long to figure out that when you shoot a bird, his job is to find it and bring it to you. Sparky—and this goes for most Sparkys— *loves* to play fetch.

Having said that, I need to add this:

A "fetch" command is useless unless the dog has been force-trained to retrieve. Otherwise, it's like an "eat" command when you put a bowl of food in front of him. If he feels like eating, you don't need a command. If he doesn't, you can stand there and say "eat" until next Sunday, but he probably isn't going to obey. You haven't taught him to obey "eat" any more than you've taught him to "fetch" by throwing the ball that he wanted thrown in the first place. You don't have a command, you have a cheer.

My setter Stella was Sparky with the ball. She never needed to be taught, and she retrieved every grouse and woodcock I shot over her during her first season. But I have a photo sequence of her taken in December 1989. That's her, swimming across a river and climbing onto the shelf ice on the other side. That's her, walking to the black duck I had shot. And that is her, too, looking back at me with an expression that says, "You want me to fetch *this?* Are you kidding?"

The photos that I *don't* have of that subfreezing day are of me walking well upstream and getting wet in order to make my own retrieve of that duck.

A dog that has been force-trained to retrieve will fetch anything he's told to fetch—a goose, a pheasant, a beer can, a rock. Further, the process of force-training produces a series of routines that can immediately be used as a fast one-minute refresher course in the field to get a nonperforming dog back to par.

Although I haven't had a lot of luck teaching it, the NAVHDA (North American Versatile Hunting Dog Association) folks have a step-by-step method that has worked for some of my hunting partner's dogs.

I just wish I had missed that duck.

In the tall grass I nearly missed Winnie's point. She had a pheasant, but as pheasants so often do, this one slipped out as I approached. Winnie moved ahead, cautiously at first, then faster when the bird reached the bordering alders and began to run in earnest. I moved to cut him off, but the rooster flushed using the alders as a screen. I fired the tight barrel at him and he flipped over in the air, wing hit. We hurried to the spot where he came down. Winnie circled once when I told her to "Find dead" then took off down the brush-lined stream course at a run. I followed as best I could, but upright critters are not meant to move quickly through alder runs, and soon I could no longer hear Winnie's bell.

The thick stuff ended where the stream emptied into an open meadow. I looked, but my dog was nowhere to be seen. It was 1979, and there was no other dog in the world that I would have rather had chasing down a cripple for me than Winnie. Her years of experience and her unusual persistence made her better at it than any dog I'd known. Given that, perhaps the wise thing to do would have been to sit down and await her return. But when five minutes had passed, my thoughts began to run to the muskrat traps I had sometimes found along brooks such as this one. I began searching and was soon knee-deep in the swamp.

Far off—so far away that at first I didn't connect the distant motion with what I was searching for—I saw her.

Win had been gone for only ten minutes, but it seemed like hours. As she approached I could see that her head was held at a labored angle under the burden she carried, but her step was deliberate and she came to me and stretched high to deliver to my hand a pheasant that had been destined to be a lost bird from the moment I pulled the trigger.

A lot has been written about dogs refusing to retrieve woodcock. I've never owned a dog that wouldn't. But—and I think there's a connection here—I've never had a hardmouthed dog either.

What's hardmouth, you say?

Sparky is supposed to retrieve birds with his mouth, but he's not supposed to sample them. A dog that likes to chomp on birds will soon discover that woodcock are loosely feathered and very bloody, and that they tend to leave undesirable residuals in a dog's mouth. Doves are pretty much the same.

Hardmouth can be a real problem. The same explosion of intensity that causes a dog to charge forward at the flush can also cause him to be hardmouthed. So can playing tug of war. Or letting the dog keep—and subsequently chew up—the things you use as retrieving dummies.

Whatever its cause, one thing is certain: hardmouth is a problem without an easy cure. Reprimanding the dog for crunching the bird might send the wrong signal; he's in the middle of doing something that's *mostly* right, after all. Sparky might end up thinking, "Okay, maybe he doesn't want the bird brought in after all. Instead, I'll bury it."

Put pins in the dummy. Wrap the bird in barbed wire. Make the dog retrieve rocks. All of those are cures that don't work. The only thing they do is teach Sparky, who's not stupid, not to chew on any bird that has first been wrapped in barbed wire.

I've used scrub brushes as retrieving dummies on the theory that the bristles hurt the dog's gums if he bites too hard on it. I've also used pheasant wings, since there's nothing there for him to chomp on besides old feathers and dried up skin. But I wouldn't put much stock in either of them as hardmouth cures. Instead, I put my faith in prevention measures. For puppies, no chewing on retrieved items and no tug of war. And in the field, keep the dog calm and under control instead of letting him charge ahead at the flush.

Here, more than in any other aspect of training, you're doing something the dog likes to do. He will be as good at retrieving as you insist he be; you can insist that he sit to deliver, and you can insist that he not sample the birds as he brings them in.

But you have to insist.

Although we all like to tell stories about old dogs teaching young dogs, incidents of an old dog teaching a young one anything useful are rare. I said as much in the first chapter. So maybe this is a case of the exception proving the rule.

Old Duffy allowed a puppy to get away with stealing his points for an entire spring. (The pup was Winnie, the dog making the retrieve earlier in this chapter.) Maybe the old dog excused it on the idea that "she's just a puppy." But as soon as hunting season started, Duffy somehow realized we were playing for keeps. When Winnie tried to move in front, Duffy growled a warning, and when that went unheeded, he grabbed her by the neck and wrestled her to the ground.

Duffy was the sort of dog that would stay ticked-off for the rest of the day, so a morning's hunt pretty much went up in smoke. I wasn't happy. But for as long as she lived I never again had a problem with Winnie honoring another dog's point.

Older dogs usually serve best in the demonstration phase of training. They know how to do it, after all. My older dog Amy proved this recently during a training session I was having with my newest pup Sophie.

I had gotten through the first "go fetch" lessons and was trying to teach the puppy to deliver a scrub brush to my hand rather than drop it just before she got to me. Amy watched from the kennel, eager to have her turn at a game she always enjoyed. After a dozen unsuccessful puppy retrieves, I let Amy out and and placed the puppy in the kennel. It was one of those what-the-hell impulses.

While the puppy watched, Amy fetched the brush to my hand several times. I made a big show of being pleased when she would sit to deliver. Then I let the puppy out, and I swear, on the first toss she imitated Amy and did it exactly right.

Sometimes, when people see the things bird dogs do in the field, they ask me questions. One of my favorite goes like this: "What do you *do* to that dog to make him hunt like that? Punish him? Run him until he drops? Beat him?"

Now I realize that people who ask that sort of thing are usually the kind who put clothes on their pets. And, admittedly, someone would have to use a whip on *me* to get me to run around the way my dogs do. That may explain their question, but it also explains why I prefer bird dogs to most people.

I've known intelligent men who believe the best way to train a dog is just to take him hunting. "I want to enjoy my dog," they'll say, "and have him be part of the good times I'm going to have. Why make work out of something that's supposed to be fun?"

While I'd be the first to agree with the "fun" part, thinking an untrained dog is smart enough to figure it out is almost always a mistake.

With that in mind, I've become a great believer in an approach that I call, for want of a better name, the "shotgun method." It's the shotgun method because everything is done in one shot, followed by everything in another shot, followed by yet another shot of everything. Think of it as an accelerated training method.

First, do the necessary yard training. Then, as soon as you can, get him into the field so that it all begins to mean something. The "invisible leash of obedience" now gives you some control over him, and allows you to begin making progress in the field from day one. Along the way to becoming a law-abiding dog, Sparky should have learned a thing or two about taking instruction. If so, when you correct him he should figure, "Hey, if the big guy wants me to stay in front of him, I'll give it a try." He's got a lot to learn in a short time, so the only way you can be successful with the shotgun method is by following the advice I gave in the last chapter: "Never permit your dog to do anything you will later have to teach him *not* to do."

There is no real secret to the shotgun method, just working it out. If you're willing to uphold your part of the bargain, a puppy can hunt, point, and retrieve in his first season. Oh, he'll do a better job of it in his second year, and better yet in his third, but we're hunting with our dogs from the very beginning. That's what it's all about. In training, there is always a temptation to follow a formula. Books written by men far more experienced than I describe a training method that dictates specific times and sequences for training a bird dog:

> *In his first year, the dog should do this, but not that... In his derby year, introduce this... A dog should not be taught such and such until he is steady to wing and shot.*

I used to think it was all true, but I'm not so sure anymore. I've become an evangelist for the shotgun approach.

To me, formula training smacks of assembly-line techniques and is only logical when several dozen dogs are being trained at once. It is a method that requires dogs to fit the mold. Dogs that don't are culls.

The methods of the pros are not designed for amateurs, but are packaged and sold to us anyway. As proof, I have a couple dozen such books on my own shelf. (The only one I pay much attention to anymore, as I mentioned earlier, is Wolters' *Gun Dog*.) I'm not disputing that the famous pro who wrote the book does a good job. But all he can prove is that his methods work for *him*.

Me, I train my dogs one at a time. I'm skeptical of any training book that contains photos of more than one puppy being worked at once, or of a trainer with any assistant other than his wife. Dog handlers on horses make me suspicious, as do roading harnesses and pigeons kept specifically for training. If that book is supposedly written for someone like me, they have me confused with a much wealthier man.

The local outdoor writer owns a well-bred English setter that is out of a semi-famous line of Connecticut shooting dogs. Stories in his owner's newspaper column have made the dog somewhat notorious for hunting over the horizon and disappearing for days at a time. In the hot stove league, the whole business has become something of an Aesop's fable, the moral being, "That's what happens when you buy a field-trial puppy."

Yet my own Amy is a littermate to that setter.

She might have turned out like her brother if I hadn't leaned on her, but that's not the point. The point is she didn't. And that should say a great deal to the argument about whether or not range is in a dog's blood.

Many men will excuse their dog's running wild by saying "Well, he's out of field-trial stock." Now, there are field trials and then there are field trials, but I've never seen one yet where the dog is *supposed* to run away. Corvair setters are essentially untrained dogs, regardless of what it says on their pedigrees.

With just one exception, every setter I've owned has been out of field-trial stock, albeit New England gun-dog and shooting-dog types. I've had some "hot" dogs (and Amy certainly meets that definition), but I've never had a runaway. Hey, every young dog with any snots at all is going to see how much he can get away with. Young Sparky is only following William Blake's epigram, "How are we to know what is enough unless we learn what is more than enough?" The real test is what *you* are willing to do about it. It is one of many possible undesirable behaviors that you might have to deal with, but certainly not a reason to give up on the dog. It's a problem that, initially, is not too bad but will get progressively worse unless you chase the dog down and remind him that this is more than enough.

Is range a hereditary trait? Enough folks confuse red-hot enthusiasm—and its results when unbridled—with range, so I would qualify whatever answer I gave.

Breeding certainly matters, but not in the question of "How big did the dog's parents run?" No. Breeding matters in the area of trainability. Is the puppy willing to come to terms with the idea that all this bird hunting business is a service he's providing to *you?* Is he trainable?

Some dogs have a lot of trouble with that idea. Others never need to be told.

A puppy might investigate a piece of cover in any of several manners. Some see only the far side and blast through with the afterburners going, others want to investigate every scent, still others don't want to stray far from their master.

To define hunt/search, bring the same dog back after he's hunted for a half-dozen seasons and had a couple hundred birds shot over him. Our jet-propelled puppy, the one that shot through the cover, might not have slowed down, but he'll take a route along the downwind side of the line of thick stuff, and he might make a long diagonal cast across that open area rather than running a straight line.

The other puppy, the one that tried to be in all places at the same time, has figured out where the most productive places are likely to be. He can be seen alternately sprinting as he bypasses things that would have held his attention a few seasons earlier, then slowing to investigate a margin just long enough to draw a conclusion before sprinting to the next likely corner.

And the third puppy, the one who seemed torn between the desire to explore and the need to stay close, has become a bold and tireless hunter. He casts back and forth in a sixty-yard windshield wiper imitation that covers all the ground in front of his master.

Each dog has developed his own style of hunting. By comparing the dog to the puppy he used to be, it soon becomes evident that hunting is not just running, and searching is not just covering ground, although the terms are often mistakenly interchanged. Hunt/search is a dog learning to adjust his speed to match the cover and the range of his nose. Also, it's the dog learning to by-pass nonproductive areas while seeking out the sort of places that have proven birdy in the past. It's a dog hunting within the confines of range and pattern. And it's a dog intelligently using the wind. Hunt/search is a bird dog spending his energy wisely.

Most astounding of all, it's a skill that the dog teaches himself. For me—a hunter, dog owner, and outright fan of bird dogs—the whole process holds a fascination as it unfolds. But the dog trainer part of me is frightened by it for the same reason: *The dog teaches himself.* Oh, as trainers we can direct him and encourage him when he's done right, but mostly it is his own successful and unsuccessful experiences that show him the correct way. The best we can do is take him out as much as possible. After all, he's not going to learn hunt/search without a fair amount of hunting and searching.

If hunt/search is what a good bird dog does when he does not have birds, then the definition of bird sense encompasses all the things he does once a bird is found. Similarly, if "just running" is not hunting, then "just smelling" is certainly not bird sense.

Scotch-taped inside my hunting journals over the years are hundreds of photos of my dogs on point. *So-and-so false pointing in such-and-such a covert* is the gist of what I've written under many of them. Yet it strikes me now as it always did—the dog might have been wrong, but she wasn't lying. When working scent, dogs—particularly young dogs—make mistakes. If they could, they'd probably be the first to admit it. Sometimes they work rabbits or mice or old scent, or they trail the wrong way. Or they simply fail—the bird eludes them. Dogs screw up. But, unlike humans, they never lie about it.

Bird sense doesn't come easy. Think of it. To pin a bird, a dog must approach close enough so that the bird is too frightened to run, yet not so frightened that it takes wing. Puppies simply point; an experienced dog will realize that he is communicating with you when he does. That comes with bird sense. Bird sense is knowing when a bird is moving and then knowing what to do about it. It's an educated nose that can differentiate between old and new scent, between foot and body scent, a nose that can handle a covey of quail and then, moments later, do a workmanlike job on the scattered singles. Like hunt/ search, it's a skill that the dog figures out pretty much on his own.

I described a training method of lifting a puppy's head so he'll learn to find woodcock by body scent rather than following the often confusing but far stronger foot scent that little Mr. Knuckleball trails behind him. To learn from that head-lifting exercise, the puppy has to find birds. Picking his head up becomes a pointless exercise if the dog cannot equate that high-headed posture with fruitful results.

I'm sure there are similar little tricks in training a dog to find sharptails or bobwhites or whatever bird you're hunting in your neck of the woods. Whatever the trick, you need birds—wild birds—if the dog is to develop bird sense. Planted pigeons and pen-raised quail are fine for "Introduction to Bird Work 101," but for all his other college courses a bird dog needs to hunt for things that are trying hard not to be found. To react naturally, a bird must be in its own environment, and that's the very same classroom in which Sparky needs to succeed and fail, over and over, before he can ever graduate from the school of bird sense.

Training is what we give to the dog. Education is what the dog does with that training. And bird sense is what he then does with that education. It's bird sense that makes bird dogs. Unfortunately, it all takes time. Someone—I think it was me—once said that right around the time dogs get it all figured out, they die of old age.

By way of definition, a dog that is "steady to wing and shot" is one that won't move after the bird is flushed and killed. In training terminology, such a dog is said to be "broke." It's one of the few things we teach that is completely contrary to what the dog wants to do. As such, you won't get many arguments that it's not only the most difficult to teach, but also the toughest to hang onto once taught. That leads to some interesting conversations:

"Sparky used to be broke, but he ain't now."

"So he's fixed?"

"No—'course not."

"But you said he's not broke anymore?"

"It's a damn shame."

"So how are you going to repair the damage?"

"I'll break him."

"I see. And who's on first?"

That steadiness business, in it's extreme, takes on a great deal of importance in field trials. In an arena where *all* of the dogs can find and point *all* of the birds, it gives the judges one more criterion to judge.

But to a hunter, it is one of those refinements that we don't want to pay extra for.

At the opposite extreme from a "broke" dog is one that chases birds once they are flushed. (This type dog is known as a Corvair setter—unsteady to wing, shot, and icy pavement at any speed.) Some hunters will say that they actually *want* their dogs to do just that, since a dog that makes the retrieve without being told will get to down-but-not-out birds before they can scurry into hiding. As long as the dog has found the bird, what does it matter if he chases?

There are arguments for both sides, but it's interesting that the dog's habit of chasing seems to be more a matter of default than something he was trained to do. In truth, we've all had to pass up low shots because a chasing dog was included in the sight picture. And when the flushed bird is the first of several, those second and third birds are usually bumped up when the dog charges out after the flushed bird. Quail, of course, are usually found in multiples and can be counted on to fly low. A dog that chases might just as well stay home.

But my chief objection goes like this: It's not that permitting the dog to chase is in and of itself so bad. No—it's what it inevitably leads to. If the pointed bird can be seen to move, sooner or later Sparky will begin to interpret that movement as the flush. And if "flush" has come to mean "chase," then quite suddenly you don't have a pointing dog any longer.

Amy was and is trained, and she doesn't chase birds. But if I let her, at the flush she'll go crazy for a minute or two, running aimlessly like an exploding mainspring from one of the wristwatches I was going to repair when I was a kid. That craziness is a pain in the neck; I have to round her up, calm her down, then send her to make a retrieve that may have started out being routine but by now may have become something more. It's a bad news/bad news situation.

Some dogs only need to be taught once. Amy is the other type of dog, the kind that "used to be broke." God knows, I've tried everything with her. Training will take but won't stick for very long. The Amy-type dog needs to be constantly "leaned on."

What to do?

In Amy's case, I lean on her.

But a bird hunter faces a dilemma: he needs to be concerned with bird shooting at the same moment he also needs to be concerned with dog training. (This is part of the explanation as to why I'm usually proud of my two-year-old dogs and very often at odds with my six- and seven-year-olds.) So we compromise. A chasing dog is a dog out of control. This, at the exact time when we might require maximum performance from Sparky. Somewhere between the two extremes a bird dog can be taught not to chase by insisting that he never be more than a command away from being brought to a halt.

It's all a matter of that "whoa" command again.

In bird dog training, there are a lot of problems, but give gun shyness and deer chasing all the attention you would contagious and incurable diseases. Both are easy to catch and impossible to cure. I say incurable because I personally know of no bird dog that has ever been completely rid of either of those problems once it has taken hold. Oh, I'm sure somewhere someone has resolved one or the other so that normal operations can resume, but that's not the issue. For you and me, gun shyness and deer chasing are incurable. That means the only solution is prevention.

Unlike most other dog-training difficulties, once we have a gun shy dog, we amateurs can't say, "Hold on a minute—let's back up and start over." The dog has not "learned" to be gun shy, any more than a person has "learned" to be claustrophobic. Subjecting the dog to more gunfire in the hopes he'll get used to it can only make the problem worse.

A solution? Since he didn't decide to be gun shy, he cannot now be taught not to be. A trainer can't work with a part of the dog's mind that the dog himself has no control over. Some men claim to have a cure; none will guarantee it.

But I will.

My "cure" involves understanding what causes gun shyness and not letting it happen in the first place. Puppies are cute and curious and a lot of fun, but because they have no body of experience to fall back upon, they are easily frightened by anything new. The Fourth of July can be a terrifying time for a wide-eyed puppy that can't understand all the noise. So can a trip to the skeet range.

Dog training books are full of methods on how you might gradually introduce him to gunfire. In truth, they all work. *But you have to do it.* All you need is a little boy's cap pistol and a belief in the steady-strain theory of dog training. This is not the sort of thing you can let go until later. For that matter, a .22 blank pistol is a necessity for field training—you might as well invest in one early on.

Here's another time when an older dog's presence will help. At feeding time, the pistol goes off and the puppy says, "What the hell was that!" He looks around and Old Sparky hasn't even looked up from his feed pan. The puppy figures that whatever it was, it can't be too bad if Sparky Senior didn't bat an eye.

Chasing deer is the other serious problem where an ounce of prevention is truly the only cure. I've never read or heard of a cure for deer chasing that seemed believable. Even the dog writer I respect as the ultimate guru of all things bird doggie pretty much fell flat when he tried to explain a cure for deer chasing. I don't know what the right answer is, or even if one exists. What I do know for certain is that every bird dog I've ever known that was allowed to get into the deer chasing habit is either dead or still doing it.

Like so many other things the dog teaches himself, if you never let him take the first lesson, the problem can be avoided. Being able to control the dog's range is part of the answer. And the "stop" command has to carry some weight.

There's that "whoa" thing again.

The longer I know dogs, the more certain I am that they *think* but can't *reason*—at least, not in a way that makes them capable of understanding why certain acts or habits might result in punishment. What they do understand is being caught in the act and smacked for it. That works.

No matter how loud their owner yells, most dogs won't whoa if they're on the hot scent of a running pheasant.

But mine will.

That's not a brag, and it's not because they're better than other dogs or because they're more intelligent. They stop because a long time ago Frank Roach told me how to make my commands stick. He said, "Go make that dog wish he had stopped when you told him to." Is that a training secret? I hope not.

A good field habit to get into involves putting the dog through his paces when you first step out of the truck: heel, whoa, come, heel, go ahead, whoa, heel. It's always on my New Year's resolution list—I don't do it enough. Sparky needs to practice that routine for the same reason infielders throw the ball around before each inning. Not to learn anything—hell, they all know how to throw and catch—but to remind themselves (and their arms and gloves) what they're there for. That's what warm-ups are all about. At a time when he's most excited, you need to give Sparky a mental wake-up call and put him through a short obedience routine.

Dogs love to hunt, and I've gotten results by taking the hunt part away—that is, putting the dog at heel when he misbehaves. In the right situation during the "enforcement" part of his lessons afield, wonderful things can happen in a very short time.

Problem: You chase the dog, the dog runs away. A stock solution is to attach a check cord to his collar. When the time comes, you needn't catch the dog, only his check cord. That sounds good, but unfortunately most of us amateur trainers have given up on the idea because the cord inevitable tangles itself and catches on every bush and snag, with a net result of very little training per unit of aggravation.

To overcome the problem, make your check cord from cheap clothesline—the hollow plastic kind is best. It is smooth and resists knotting. You'll have a cord that will slip easily past snags, yet will be there when you need to pull an overzealous puppy to a halt.

As an appendix to that idea, I might add that it's important that you get started with the check cord *before* you need it. That way, the puppy is used to wearing it whenever you go afield.

A question often asked of dog trainers is, "Should I put a shock collar on my dog?" The answer involves an understanding of what the collar can and cannot do; it also involves a good deal of judgment.

The same technology that gave us the automatic garage door opener and the remote TV channel changer has produced a method for giving a dog a long-distance kick in the pants. Certainly, men have effectively trained dogs since long before the shock collar was invented. Excessive range, running up birds, and other field problems were addressed and corrected. The offending dog would be chased down and returned to the scene of the crime where a correction was administered. That is still the preferred non-electronic method of teaching at a distance.

In my younger days, I did my share of running down and rounding up, too. Yet, in retrospect, I'm sure that as often as not, by the time I caught up with the dog *he had no idea what he was being punished for.*

Enter "the hammer."

On the surface, the immediate and long-distance effect of the modern electronic training collar seems like a short-cut to solving any of several dog-training problems. "Immediate," since at the heart of all obedience training is the doggie equation that says, "I do this, I get that." The collar can eliminate the time lapse between "this" and "that."

The long-distance part is the other key. Dog training, and all its inherent ramifications, boils down to controlling the situation. Getting Ol' Sparky to do what he should when you're not there to physically make him do it is a control problem. The collar is a long-distance control solution.

I'm fond of saying that, as bird dog trainers, all we do is establish margins. That means that field training a bird dog becomes an elaborate game of "you're getting hotter—now you're getting colder..." The shock collar lets him know when he's really freezing.

The electronic training collar is a cure for disobedience. But what it's *not,* is as important as what it is. Realize that the collar cannot teach a dog anything positive—it can only undo negative traits. Ol' Sparky must know what is right and wrong before you ever put the hammer on him, and that implies a good deal of judgment on the part of you, the trainer. Is Ol' Sparky disobedient? Or is it more a matter of him not being trained thoroughly enough? It is a rare dog that doesn't have to be shown something more than once, and many need a lot of repetition. Have you done your part?

I have seen dogs ruined permanently by the injudicious use of a shock collar. So have you. Like anything potent, it can be abused. Here are some guidelines as recommended by the Mulak Institute of Corrective Dog Behavior:

1. *Never* use the collar when you're angry at the dog.

2. *Never* use the collar if there is any doubt that the dog knows what you want him to do and that he heard you tell him to do it.

3. Accompany each use with a command, so that the dog knows what he's being zapped for.

4. Continue to use physical correction whenever possible so that the shock doesn't become the *only* form of punishment the dog receives. Be sure the dog knows it's *you* rather than the collar that is doing the reprimanding.

5. The shock collar makes your whip hand longer. Be sure that the same thing happens to the *other* hand, the one you use to pat him on the head when he's done a good job.

6. And finally, a good trainer knows when to be forgiving of dog's mistakes. Be careful that you don't become a fanatic about it all. As irritating as an untrained dog might be, there are few things more cheerless and pathetic than an overtrained dog.

Should you put a shock collar on your dog?

Some dogs are equally obedient at short and long distances and seem to train themselves. Count yourself blessed if this describes your dog, and spend your money elsewhere.

Some behavior problems have more to do with maturity than disobedience; in a year or two the dog may outgrow whatever it is that bothers you.

And consider the consensus among dog trainers that most dogs need a good deal more time afield than they get; Sparky's problem may have more to do with inexperience than disobedience.

To be sure, there are other methods of curing field problems, some of them time-proven. But for anything that requires immediacy at a long distance, there is nothing so positive as the immediate wake-up call provided by the collar. When used properly, the electronic training collar works as advertised, quickly correcting unwanted behavior.

In the last chapter I asked the question, "How good a bird dog do you want?" The answer for most of us would not be the jet-propelled field-trial champion. Although we might *want* such a dog, since we're in the business of making our own bird dogs, we simply don't see the investment in time and effort as as being worth the results. If the speed limit is 55, why do I want a speedometer that goes to 120?

So how much less? How much dog is good enough for you? What would Sparky have to become to make you happy? Again, the question inevitably takes a pragmatic turn and becomes, "How good a bird dog are you willing to pay for?" Understand that we amateur dog trainers are paying for this ideal dog with time and effort, not cash.

With an older dog—that is, a dog that's not an untrained puppy anymore—you must make up your mind specifically what it is that you want to accomplish. What is it that you don't like about what he's doing? What would it take to make you happy? Total improvement in an older dog—completely eliminating all his bad habits—might be more that you can handle alone. You might consider putting Sparky with a professional trainer. If pros have an advantage, it is having successfully been through the whole business before, and having the confidence that it can be done again.

But before Ol' Sparky can change (and before anything that a pro might change can become permanent) it's *you* who must change your methods. If there is a yin and yang in bird dog training, it is in the idea that Sparky will be as good as you insist he be, while being as bad as you're willing to tolerate. Whatever happens externally to the dog won't do any good if *you* are not willing to become insistent.

The first dog that ever tried to teach me anything was a liver-and-white Brit named Duffy. Among the things I learned was that there wasn't much of anything he wouldn't do for a dog biscuit, and not just the fetch-heel-stay sort of things, either; he would jump up in the air, dance around, even sing—after a fashion. That was his "handle," so I used to carry Milk Bones in the pocket of my hunting jacket. Occasionally I used them to reward the dog, but more often than not they permitted me to eat my own lunch without having to share it with the bottomless pit that was Duffy's appetite for people food. If you've ever tried to give a begging dog "just one little piece" of a ham and cheese sandwich, you'll know what I'm talking about.

One November morning Duffy and I were hunting the edge of a swamp in Amherst. After some false pointing and a good deal of running back and forth, a stocked pheasant took wing out of gunshot range. I knew it was a stocked bird because it landed in the top of a flimsy sapling about sixty yards away and nearly bent the tree top over. From its tentative perch the bird watched the dog and me.

I was young enough to consider shooting the bird as he sat there, but old enough to have been disgusted when I'd seen others do the same. So I shook the little tree in an attempt to get the bird to fly. He held on with both feet, and gave me a "Hey—no fair!" look.

I searched around for a rock to throw, but discovered they're hard to come by in a swamp. I couldn't even find a decent stick. So I threw a shotgun shell, and then another. Both missed, and I didn't see where they came down. A third throw had similar results. I was running out of ammo, but still hadn't fired my gun. Meanwhile, the bird continued to watch intently. I knew the pheasant wasn't a rocket scientist, but still, I was afraid to put the gun down, knowing for certain that that would be when he'd take off.

I didn't have enough ammo to continue my inaccurate David and Goliath routine, so I started throwing dog biscuits. I used the unbroken ones—they seemed to have more heft. After several missed throws, I noticed Duffy running in circles on the far side of the tree. My attention was still on the pheasant, so I didn't think much of it until I noticed him leap about three feet in the air: he was catching the biscuits before they could fall back to the ground. I went over and kicked him in the butt.

Finally, the next Milk Bone hit the bird squarely in the head and ricocheted high into the air. The pheasant seemed to consider that for a moment, then fell out of the tree and hit the ground like a sack of potatoes.

Duffy, well-trained and loyal hunting companion that he was, stood waiting for my command. When I sent him to fetch, he leaped right over the pheasant and went directly to the spot where the fatal dog biscuit had landed. I might add that he didn't offer me even one little piece.

This story is not without a moral, of course, and there is an obvious dog training lesson here: When hunting, be sure to carry only *whole* dog biscuits. Personally, I'd recommend the "beagle/cocker spaniel" size for smaller upland birds, but move up to "collie/German shepherd" size for pheasants and waterfowl.

And don't spend too much time looking for pellets when cleaning out your birds.

Few battle plans ever survive their first contact with the enemy.

Ulysses S. Grant

"Dog hair!" she said. She made it sound like something you wouldn't want to step in while wearing new shoes.

Attributed to
Steven Mulak's mother

five

The Other
Ten Months

Some folks moved in next door to us a few years back. They had a mongrel who spent virtually all his time engaged in the canine sport of recreational barking. The dog's voice, while not unusually loud, had an amazing carrying quality to it that endeared him to neighbors several streets away.

After observing that I had a pair of relatively silent dogs in my yard, the new neighbor asked what she might do about Duke. I suggested an antibark collar. Back then, they went for about fifty bucks. "It gives the dog a little electric shock each time he barks," I told her. "A smart dog will stop barking in a matter of minutes, and even the dumbest dog in the world will figure he'd better shut up within a day or two."

The lady looked horrified. Oh no, she said. An electric shock sounded much too cruel.

A month later, shortly after the town dog warden had paid his second visit to their house in response to complaints from the rest of the dogless neighborhood, I noticed The Duke of All Barkers had disappeared. When I inquired, I was told they had taken him to the animal shelter. That meant he was gone for good.

"I guess it's all a matter of perspective," I said. "You see, to me, that sounds cruel, but I'll bet ol' Duke preferred being gassed to the antibark collar any day."

My wife often wonders why our relationship with those neighbors never got off the ground.

Dogs have a number of irrational habits, and attempting to address those habits with a rational solution is nearly always a mistake. Dogs don't bark because they want to be bad. Hollering out the window at a barking dog is just a temporary fix, and hoping the dog will grow out of it isn't even that. There is no rational answer to why dogs deliberately make noise. Nor to why they eat their own turds. Or why they dig holes in every corner of the yard, pee on fire hydrants, roll in cow flops, cold-nose-it with other dogs, or chew up the rose bush you just paid $19.95 for.

Dogs can be cured of irritating habits, but the more irrational the problem, the more it defies rational solutions. Dogs are not people; they are not rational beings. And although dog owners will readily agree to that statement, most domestic canine difficulties arise when dog problems are addressed with people solutions.

My solutions involve persistence and the employment of a technique that Robert Wehle, in his book *Wing and Shot*, describes as the "mild use of the flushing whip"— except that I use a plastic whiffleball bat. Duke's owner, a kind-hearted and reasonable lady, would not approve of my methods. But if she had had a viable alternative, The Duke of All Barkers would have become Duke the Silent and would still be living in the next yard.

If you have a dog, you have to come to terms with the idea that elegant landscaping and bird dogs just don't go together. For a while, we all fight it; we put wire mesh on the ground around plantings to keep the dog from digging, and we put up little fences that are supposed to keep him out of the shrubs. Sure they will.

Because neither dogs nor people ever essentially change, you can look forward to having the same fights with your dog for a long time. The unfortunate truth of the matter is that you are not going to have a yard that looks like something out of *Better Homes and Gardens*. (Privately, I think all those types of magazines are dangerous. My wife used to tear out pictures of patios and flower borders and tack them to my bulletin board. "Hints," she used to call them. Sometimes, the photos would show a cocker spaniel or a basset hound, the subliminal suggestion being that this could be the yard of any American family. Right. In rebuttal, I started tacking up a few things that I had ripped out of *Playboy*.)

Weeds were never strangers to my lawn. Prospering out there was the standard assortment of crabgrass, chickweed, creeping Charlie, and a half-dozen other undesirables whose names I'd have to look up. But until a few years ago, there was never any nutgrass. That's the coarse, bright-green stuff. In hot weather it grows so fast that two days after mowing it's sticking up again, making the lawn look worse than if you hadn't mowed in the first place. There was never any of it in the lawn until I was forced into finding a new place to exercise the dogs (an industrial park made a sudden appearance at my regular spot). Nutgrass, it seems, has a burlike seed that becomes entangled in the fur of animals, including gun dogs. And the new place was full of it. Thus, as part of nature's plan, the botanical weed patch that I pass off as a lawn now has nutgrass growing among the dandelions.

Because dogs like to run, there will be areas where you cannot grow grass. Period. In the early years of base-ball, groundskeepers were quick to stop seeding areas where they couldn't grow turf anyway. Instead, in the highest traffic areas they purposely created the now-familiar bare dirt base-paths. After a while, we dog owners begin to understand the inherent logic in that.

Be suspicious of any photo that contains a dog house with grass growing around it. Dog owners know better. The area immediately around any real-life dog house looks like an artillery practice range. The only way most dog owners' yards would ever make it into the glossy pages of *House and Garden* would be as the before part of a before-and-after photo spread. Whether you use a kennel, a fenced-in yard, or the chain-'em-to-the-dog-house method, you can't escape the fact that all dogs tend to reduce their quarters to the lowest denominator. Wild canines do the very same thing. I've seen fox dens; they look like the area around my back steps. Summer is the worst time. Dogs dig. They chew. They lift their legs. They run until they've worn a path right down to the bed rock. And when they finish, they dig and chew some more.

And if the dog lives in the house with you, you are, in his eyes at least, living in his kennel with him.

I never believed that. Not even after years of proving to myself that it was true. Thinking back, 99 percent of the problems I had with my dogs were of the domestic variety. I didn't have trouble with them when we were hunting, but it seemed I was forever ticked-off about one of them chewing up a shoe or piddling in the cellar. There was always something.

Winnie ate anything that was, is, or might in any way be related to food—the cheese in mousetraps, a used wax paper bag, a recently shot drake mallard (including the feet).

Until the day she died, Hazel used to love to chew photographs. (She was obviously an iconoclast in a previous existence.)

Zelda wasn't with us long, but I still have the Zelda Memorial Extension Cord and the Zelda Memorial Euonymus Bush and the Zelda Memorial Sheetrock Job on the cellar stairs.

Amy, on her best day, is still only about 80 percent housebroken.

Then there was Duffy. The first time—the very first time, mind you—that he entered the kitchen of our new house he lifted his leg on the refrigerator. I did some yelling and jumping up and down, but Duff was always cool. He acted like he didn't hear me and walked away from the fridge and peed on the leg of the table.

That was twenty-five years ago. You can observe my wife's reaction at the time by reminding her of it today. But I wouldn't if I were you.

For some folks, the answer to the never-ending litany of canine domestic problems is a kennel. I resisted it for a long time, but did the deed a few years ago. It's a good news/bad news situation. You get your house back because the kennel becomes the dog's home. But too many people use a kennel as a prison, letting the dog out only when he is needed. Don't permit that to happen. Let them out each time you go in the yard, and be sure it's at least twice a day.

Everybody seems happy. Now that my dogs live in their own kennel without me, whenever I go outside they are glad to see me. And I'm glad to see them. Oh, they'll still dig a hole in the corner of the yard when I'm not looking, and Amy is not above peeing in the cellar if I bring her in for an especially cold night, but compared to the parade of problems we used to have, life is good.

There are many good ideas on how and where to put your kennel, especially if you live in the suburbs. Just about every bird dog magazine I've ever picked up has an article about the dos and don'ts of kennel building. They all tell you to run water to the kennel, and to make the dog house accessible from the outside. My property is bordered on the back by oak woods. That's significant in that the floor of the forest is thickly carpeted with oak leaves, and turds thrown into the woods filter down and are never seen again. And, boy oh boy, do those oak trees grow!

One evening, six dogs ago, I was installing a lock on my front door and trying to finish before the eleven o'clock news. When Winnie wanted out I let her onto the front lawn instead of taking her through the cellar to the fenced back yard. From where I was working on the porch, I thought I could keep an eye on her.

Since I was dealing with me, I should have known better.

When next I looked up, she was out on the street, illuminated by the oncoming headlights of a car. For a terrible moment, I didn't know whether to call her and have her run in front of the car, or to take my chances that she could dodge the fenders by herself.

I should have called her.

When the car passed, she was lying in the road. I ran to her, picked her up, and put her on the floor of my truck. I yelled to my wife to call the vet and drove off into the night, running every red light I came to.

That Brittany seemed to be under the protection of a guardian angel all through her life, and in an encounter that would have killed another dog, Winnie had merely been knocked unconscious. Half way to the vet's office she woke up and found herself in the truck with me driving. She assumed we were going hunting. She sat up, looked around, and smiled her dog's smile at me, Mr. Responsibility. I felt like pulling over and smacking her for giving me such a scare, but when I stopped the truck all I could do was hug her and whisper a few thankful prayers.

Whenever any of us pick out a puppy from a litter, we take on the responsibility of looking after him for as long as he's alive. I try to keep my dogs away from all trouble by keeping them kenneled within my fenced-in back yard, but at times that's a mixed blessing. Neighborhood dogs who run loose weave in and out of traffic seemingly with impunity, but a non-street-wise dog is in grave danger near any road. I've had one dog killed and two others struck by automobiles. That statistic proves nothing, except that a dog should be taught to stay off the road. Unfortunately, I don't know how to teach that; the road is where running is easiest, and, once on their own, all dogs inexorably gravitate to it. All I can advise is be careful.

Dogs shed. If you have dogs, dog hair is a fact of life. You avoid dark-colored furniture, and learn not to pet Ol' Sparky when you're wearing your worsted wool slacks. There are times, particularly during the summer months, when you can get handfuls of hair out of your dog's coat virtually anytime, even if you've just finished combing him. I've never tried it, but I believe that in July you can comb your dog bald.

Nobody likes fleas. But flea powder works, and normal hygiene in regard to Ol' Sparky's bedding will keep fleas out of the picture. There's no good reason for any dog to have fleas.

Ticks are a different story. The little suckers will get on your dog no matter what you do short of not going into woods and fields. At first, they're very tiny and appear as bits of dirt. When you do find them, they seem to be armor plated and defy crushing with a fingernail. Oh, they'll die if you put them on a cement floor and hit them hard with a claw hammer, but few things short of that will do the trick. If you don't find them, they burrow in and hang on tight. After a few days they're not so difficult to find: they become swollen with the blood they've sucked out of your dog. They seem to have an affinity for the vascular parts of a dog's body, as well as the places where he can't scratch, so look for them between the dog's toes and under his tail as well as in the more obvious spots—around his collar and the back of his neck, on his ears and near his eyes.

I hate ticks like turkeys hate Thanksgiving. They've been around for a long time, but have only recently been associated with the spread of several diseases. It is more important than ever to keep them off Ol' Sparky. Flea and tick repellents work and might be the answer for a dog that only goes out occasionally.

But for the fellow with more than one dog, the fellow who hunts more than just a little, the best solution involves a thirty-gallon plastic trash can (with a lid) and a gallon of flea and tick dip. Mix it up, keep it covered, and dunk the dogs every twelve days or so during tick season. One batch will last all through the warm months. The dogs hate it, and will go into hiding on dip day. If it seems like a great deal of trouble, it is. But it works.

When I first had dogs, the head man at the Springfield A.S.P.C.A. was a gentlemanly veterinarian named Dr. Roy. He called every dog "Baby" in a tone that gave new meaning to the word, and was one of the very few people I've met who possessed that rarest of all human commodities: wisdom. I found that out when I asked him about dog food.

"You've really got to scratch hard these days to find a brand of dog chow that isn't good. All of 'em are complete foods." He was examining the above-mentioned Winnie as he told me this. I'm unsure if this was before or after she performed her head-meets-automobile-bumper experiment.

"They have to put some sort of stabilizer in all of it to keep the fat and protein from going bad. The dry kibble, of course, has a lot more stabilizer than the canned stuff, and that makes it more difficult for a dog to break down. If what ends up on the ground looks like what you fed her yesterday, then she's not getting what she should out of that dog food.

"My shoes are probably 25 percent protein, but Miss Winnie Baby, here, could eat 'em and they'd come out the other end with the shine still on 'em." Dr. Roy had a slow blink that gave the impression that nothing in life could excite him.

He was through with his examination. He scratched Winnie behind the ears and smiled at her. She smiled back. "I'm not going to tell you what brand of dog food to use. That's up to you. But if it was me..." At this juncture, when he was about to dispense a dollop of wisdom, he wouldn't look away from the dog. Instead, he'd raise an eyebrow and glance at his target out of the corner of his eye. "But if it was me, and I was not only paying the freight but was also the guy with the shovel, I'd be sure that whatever brand I was feeding, it would have to produce something at the other end of the dog that bore a close resemblance to a Tootsie Roll."

Early in the gunning season, the combination of warm weather and soft living can quickly drain a good hunting dog. I've never seen a dog do anything out of the ordinary while his tongue was hanging out. Every dog should learn early on to drink from a water bottle. The best time to train a puppy to do that (some things are obvious but cry out to be stated) is when he's thirsty. Here in New England, there are brooks and standing water everywhere, so it hardly seems important. But no matter where you hunt, there will come a time when you'll need to water your dog right then, and if he hasn't yet figured out the water bottle trick (and if you don't make a habit of carrying one in your hunting vest) you could find yourself hunting for mud puddles instead of game birds.

Honey, a great energy supplement for dogs, is especially useful in warm weather. It is pure energy in predigested form, and it gets into your dog's bloodstream fast. To give honey to dogs while hunting, I followed somebody's tip and tried putting it into capsules I had gotten from my pharmacist, but that's a messy process. Instead, I now keep a plastic dispenser bottle in my field bag, and at each rest stop I give the dogs a few Milk Bones, onto which I've squeezed some honey. It seems to work.

Another field supplement involves a cellophane packet of moist dog food. (I think the term Gaines Burgers has become a generic name for that stuff.) On hunting days, in addition to the regular evening meal, the dog gets half a Gaines Burger packet after the first hour of work and the other half in midafternoon. The portion is small enough so that bulking is avoided, yet it pumps some extra protein into the dog at a time when he needs it most.

During hunting season, an athletic bird dog has trouble keeping weight on, so much so that by year's end he might look emaciated. When he's working hard, Sparky may burn up more calories in an hour that he does in an entire summer day lazing around the back yard. He needs lots of calories and protein, in their most accessible forms.

Cramming enough fuel into an athletic hunting dog—and then having it assimilated—presents a problem. The low-octane stuff that meets Ol' Sparky's needs during the off season isn't going to make the grade when he starts hunting. Simply feeding him more isn't the answer, since large quantities of food tend to pass through the dog undigested. And there are definite dangers involved in feeding a dog before exercise, so twice-a-day mealtimes aren't always realistic, either.

A change of diet is in order.

Meat provides both protein and calories, and if it's been canned, it doesn't need the stabilizers found in dry kibble. But sometimes even a good butcher will give you a bum steer: when you're buying "dog meat" for Ol' Sparky, read the labels. If you weren't already aware of it, the ingredients on the label are listed in descending order. If the first product on the label is "soy grits," then there are more grits in there than anything else. You wouldn't buy "chicken soup" thinking it was all chicken. Similarly, don't mistake "beef dinner for dogs" for something that is all meat.

High protein can at times be irritative and can cause diarrhea. If it comes to that, remember that chicken seems to be a far more digestible source of protein than red meat, so choose brands based on poultry rather than horse meat or beef.

If you're going to stay with a dry dog food, a good choice for an athletic dog is the "oily" type dry foods that run upwards of 28 percent protein. Or, go with puppy food, which is very high in calories. A word of caution: No matter what sort of performance food you switch to, once the gunning season is over get Sparky back on his regular diet as quickly as possible. If he's not working it off, that high-protein stuff will make him look like Jabba the Hut in a hurry.

When I was a kid, the dogs always got any meat that was starting to go bad—cold cuts or leftovers that began to smell "funny." I think it was a matter of feeling less guilty if some use could be made of the food. ("Well, at least the dogs ate it and we didn't have to throw it out.") Although my dogs at times eat things that are a lot worse than outdated pastrami, I have stopped giving them such grub. The risk may be small, but why take it? Dog food is cheap enough.

As with people, some dogs develop a more sensitive digestive system as they get older. Old dogs do well on dog food. Period. Universally, they seem to have sensitive guts—so much so that a little gravy or turkey stuffing will give them the runs. Too bad. At a time in their lives when you'd like to give them the sort of special treatment you'd like as a senior citizen, they can't handle it. You have to be mindful of the fat content and the amount of protein in their food. None of my old dogs could handle more than 5 percent fat or 20 percent protein. As long as I could refrain from doing them favors, they did fine on ordinary super-market-brand dog food.

All of which is the long version of the answer to the question of why, even in the off season, I'm fussy about what I feed my dogs. During the other, nonhunting months of the year when they're not producing birds for me, my dogs are in the business of producing fertilizer for the oak trees behind the kennel.

And I am, as I have been a long time telling you, the guy with the shovel.

At the discount store, the woman behind the cash register remarked about the price of the dog food I was buying. It was Purina Hi-Pro. Then she asked if it was any good. Now, I'll be the first to admit that there are any number of wise-ass answers to a question like that, but I like to think I've outgrown that immature stage of my life. Besides, she looked like Ann Margret. So I told her yes, it was good for my active dogs.

"I've got an eleven-month-old peekapoo. I wish I could find something to feed to my Fluffy," she said. "He's so hyper, he won't eat ordinary dog food."

"He would if he was hungry."

She smiled as she looked at me, sure I was joking.

"Eleven-month-old puppies are supposed to be hyper," I continued. "That's what puppies do. Sometimes they can't help themselves—they act like animals."

"Oh, but not like mine," she said. "He jumps and barks and chews everything, and insists on making a mess in the house—he's such a bad boy."

It began to dawn on me that I was talking about dogs, and this woman, who owned a dog, probably couldn't find Rin Tin Tin at a cat show. I should have told her about the

Mulak Institute of Corrective Dog Behavior. But as I pointed out earlier, my wise-ass days are behind me.

You've had similar conversations, I know. Conversations in the midst of which you want to reach out and shake the other person. There are people who insist on treating dogs like children—spoiled children at that. Vets will tell you the animals are not a problem—not even the ones that snarl and bite—compared to the animals' owners. The dogs of people's imaginations are cartoons. We supercivilized Americans are guilty of making up a doggie world full of kind, sensitive people who happen to be dogs. Our pet dogs are domestic animals, certainly, and they have certain human traits. But they're still animals.

People like that should own cats. Cats, at least, have the wherewithal to ignor the foolishness of their owners. None of this would have bothered me nearly as much if Fluffy's owner had looked like a sumo wrestler in drag. I just wish she had been ugly.

When you go to sea for a living, you naturally spend a lot of time away from home. For all the years I was away, my wife was more than tolerant of the dogs' barking at noises in the night. "It's good advertising," she'd say.

Some dogs are more domesticated than others. I've known bird dogs whose only interest in humans was directly proportional to the chances of that person taking them hunting. Other dogs from the very beginning seem to make a full-time hobby out of being a pet. It's a matter of disposition.

Back when I was a kid, we had a gentle English setter named Suzie. She was already a matronly old dog of five when my dad brought her home. She was not a "boy's dog" like Lassie or Ol' Yeller, but when she wasn't hunting with Dad she belonged to my brothers and me. Suzie pulled a sled out in the winter street while I pretended I was Sergeant Preston, and she loved to come to the park with us in the summer, more to cold-nose-it with the neighborhood mongrels than out of any protective instinct for her charges. She lived in the house with our family, ate table scraps, and spent her evenings in the den by the TV. After five years in a dog breeder's kennel, life at our house must have seemed like heaven.

When I was a kid, my mom was always just "my mom." But here, from this vantage point, I can see that in 1955 she was a handsome French-Canadian woman, with the sort of shape Jane Russell was referring to when she spoke of "we full-figured girls" in her ads for Playtex bras.

Evidently, this fact was not lost on Mr. Walsh down the street. He was a nice enough man. At least he always seemed happy. Whenever we saw him, my dad would shake his head and refer to him as an alki. I thought it was a nationality, like French or Polish. I noticed, too, that Mr. Walsh's eyes often bore a close resemblance to a pair of automobile headlights.

We never had air conditioning, and when the summer evenings got hot and sticky my mother would retreat to the screened-in breezeway to do the ironing. My dad worked the three-to-eleven shift in those days, but the rest of the family was out there with her, watching Navy Log or Sergeant Bilko on the old black-and-white DuMont when Mr. Walsh pulled into the driveway. He shut his car lights off, but his eyes remained on "high beam."

What did I know? I was eight. I was surprised at Mom's hysteria when she saw who it was. "Oh no! He's coming in!"

Gentle Suzie had been sleeping under the ironing board, but the fear in my mother's voice brought her out like Rin Tin Tin. Snarling and barking, she tore out the screen on the door trying to get at Mr. Walsh. She even broke a tooth in the process. Mr. Walsh may have been drunk, but he wasn't dumb. He left in a hurry.

Now, my mother was never a great fan of any hunting dog (the dog hair quote that opens the chapter is attributed to her), and Suzie was no exception. There were incidents with tomcats and lemon meringue pies underlying my mother's convictions about Suzie. But the following Saturday, Mom permitted my father no mumbling under his breath as he repaired the screen door.

And, in an unconscious but very significant change, Suzie was promoted in my mother's vocabulary from "the damn dog" to just plain "the dog."

My little dog ten years ago
Was arrogant and spry,
But she was ten years younger then,
And so, by God, was I.
...If natural law refused her wings,
That law she would defy,
For she could do unheard-of things,
And so, at times, could I.

Ogden Nash
"For a Good Dog"

six

Care and
Maintenance of the
Athletic Hunting Dog

Back in the good old days when I had hair and arches and my children, who have since become college grads, were babies, I had a dog named Duffy. I've already introduced you to him in previous chapters. He was a large liver-and-white Brittany, maybe extra-large. Duffy lived to be twelve. During his lifetime I saw him demonstrate genuine intelligence on countless occasions, and there were times when "clever" was the only term to describe his actions. Even today, I still like to tell stories about what a smart dog he was.

But then I mention porcupines and have to take it all back. When it came to porkies, Duffy was a character out of context. When Duffy was a puppy, he and a porcupine had a close encounter of the third kind. The porky had a scare, Duffy got a dozen quills in the side of his face, and I ended up with a vet bill. For all three of us, it was the first of many such encounters. After that incident, the only time Duffy got along with porkies was when they were not around. He had a full-blown love/hate relationship with them; he hated them, but at the same time he seemed to love to seek them out.

For those of you who have never actually seen a porcupine in the wild, let me say that you're not missing much. They're not going to outsmart many critters, and there's not a lot of light in their eyes. When threatened they'll bristle-up, but I've never seen one even attempt to run away. I guess Mother Nature figured if you don't have to run, why bother? Dogs get smacked by that tailfull of quills whether they're attacking a porky or just taking a curious sniff.

Duffy, in his own way, could be incredibly stupid. On subsequent engagements he would sometimes just get smacked—if we were lucky—by the porky's tail. I carried a pair of surgical clamps (nurses call them "Kelleys") and I could pull out the twenty or thirty quills that such a casual encounter would put into Duff's face.

But we weren't usually lucky. More often than not, whenever he would come across a porcupine in the woods, Duffy's thought process went along the lines of: "There's that SOB again. This time, before he gets a chance to hurt me, I'm going to bite him *real good*."

The inevitable result of such porcupine-versus-tooth-and-fang encounters was hundreds of quills in Duffy's lips, gums, tongue, the roof of his mouth—a real mess. It was more than I could handle alone, and I'd run stop signs and break speed limits to get him to the nearest vet.

Understand, I'm talking an average of twice a season with this porcupine business. People used to wonder why

I brought along my checkbook when I went hunting. Duffy's antics taught me many, many things that have helped me understand other dogs, not the least of which is: Some of the things dogs do defy understanding.

Some men, thinking they're doing all dogs a favor, will shoot every porcupine they come across in the woods. While I'm no big fan of porkies, I don't vote for that approach.

So what should you do about them?

Admittedly, anything I advise is suspect, since I just finished telling a story in which I confessed to not being able to convince a smart dog to keep away from porcupines. Having once been ignorant on this subject does not, in and of itself, make me an expert now. But I believe my Brittany was caught up in a vicious cycle—he felt an ongoing victim's right to revenge. With that in mind, if you can stop a curious pup before he ever gets himself into porky trouble, the cycle can be broken before it ever gets started.

It has worked for me in training subsequent puppies. Whenever we would come across a porcupine in the woods, I would collar the dog. If the puppy showed any interest at all, I'd smack her. Then I'd push her toward the porky, and if she took my encouragement, I'd smack her again. Invariably, each dog figured it out: "Whatever these things are, the big guy wants me to stay away from them. That's okay with me." It's a lot like breaking a dog of its natural interest in rabbits. Only easier, since rabbits won't hold still while you remind a puppy that he's not a basset hound.

After our children were born, my wife searched out a pediatrician who shared her belief in giving the body a chance to heal itself. Sometimes a doctor needs to help it along, but only sometimes. The doctor she found was not a "medicine man" who would pump drugs into the kids for every minor sniffle. Other than the few occasions when my daughters were genuinely sick and needed antibiotics, about the strongest thing he ever prescribed was baby aspirin.

Likewise, when I had to seek out a new vet, I sought a similar no-nonsense doctor who was, preferably, a bird hunter. You see, there are veterinarians (good intending people, no doubt) who will tell you not to hunt Sparky for six weeks because of some minor injury. This in the middle of hunting season! I was lucky and stumbled upon a man who, while not a hunter himself, knows why I have bird dogs and will go to great lengths to see to it that they can continue to hunt. As such, when *he* tells me to keep the dog off her cut paw for six weeks, I know it's serious and take him at his word.

Wherever game birds live, barbed wire seems to be an ever-present hazard. As recently as seventy years ago most of New England was under cultivation. Nearly all of the little hill farms have since been abandoned and have grown to grouse cover, but the barbed wire remains. It persists, strung to tree trunks and fallen fence posts, long forgotten and often unseen, but still capable of tearing a hunk out of a hunter's rubber-bottomed boot—or a bird dog's hide. Any dog that hunts grouse and woodcock in New England learns to be careful around barbed wire.

But every so often a hard-going bird dog cuts himself on the stuff. The wound is almost always in the form of a rip in the skin, and some wounds need stitches. But more often than not, the above-mentioned vet says to me, "It looks worse than it is. Just keep it clean and covered—it'll heal all by itself." It has to do with the way the cut lies when the dog is standing.

I should add that I've been running torn-up dogs to the vet for twenty-five years, and will continue to do so; I'd rather have him tell me what I know already than err in the other direction.

Dogs get sprains, strains, pulls, charley horses, and the whole assortment of other ailments we've come to associate with human athletes. The biggest problem in treating a dog for these types of injuries is that he can't tell you what hurts (at least, none of mine ever have). You have to observe the dog limping or favoring one leg to realize all is not well.

There are basically two types of strains: the one that gets better as the dog warms up, and the one that gets worse the longer the dog runs. Of the two, the first will generally heal itself. But be careful of the second type—it usually requires action on your part, and only a vet can best advise you on proper treatment.

Of the dog-will-fix-it-himself theory of veterinary medicine, I offer the following story (if I hadn't actually witnessed it in person, I'd be afraid to repeat it for fear of being accused of exaggeration). My hunting partner's dog, Bandit, cut his pad while we were out together. My partner put the dog in the back of the truck and we continued to hunt, using only my Brittany. When we returned an hour later, Bandit had made some emergency repairs and was ready to go again. His self-styled instant fix consisted of chewing off the cut part of his pad so that he could still run.

As bird dogs go, Bandit was a real lulu. The piece he had chewed off wasn't as big as a pork chop, but almost. My high school football coach would have loved that dog, since Bandit was the incarnation of his berserk philosophy of competition: "What the hell's the matter with you, Mulak? Get back in there. You're hurt? Big deal. Just bite off the broken part and keep playing...Or are you a quitter, Mulak?"

Many dog owners like to brag about their dogs being "briar busters," the implication being that the dog has a lot of heart and displays an admirable eagerness to hunt. Since most dogs eventually outgrow their kamikaze tendencies, a puppy's willingness to plunge headfirst through thorns indicates only that he has a lot to learn.

During her early years, Amy was a notorious briar buster. When it came to thorns, she didn't seem to give a damn. Her coat was not thick, but she had the other prerequisite for briar busting—a thick skull. By the end of the hunting season, most of the fur on the fronts of her legs and chest had been worn off. No kidding. If she had been made of metal, she would have been very, very shiny.

Once, during her second season, a briar cut the tip of her ear. No big deal, I thought, and we kept going. But each time she ran a step, the ear flew around like a piece of laundry in the wind, and the clotting that would have happened in any other small cut never took hold. Within five minutes her head and shoulders were covered with a fine mist of blood. Leaves and bugs were stuck to her in a big gory mess. She looked like an extra from a canine horror movie.

I got her home and washed her down in the cellar tub. I bandaged the ear tip with gauze, but I was reluctant to use adhesive tape. Anyone who has ever pulled a Band-Aid off a hairy forearm knows how excruciating that sort of pain can be. It has to be the same for dog fur. So instead, I used an Ace bandage. I carefully wrapped Amy's head so that her ear was immobilized, and I allowed just the smallest piece of adhesive tape to come in actual contact with her fur.

Amy curled up on her bed in the cellar and looked at me with love in her eyes. Even Susan made a nonsarcastic remark about me being a considerate dog owner. For one fleeting moment, I felt like Saint Francis of Assisi.

What a fool.

Two hours later, I went back into the cellar to see how Amy was doing. As all dogs are wont to do with bandages, she had pawed at it until it had come off. Of course, she had started shaking her head. And naturally, the cut had re-opened. The cellar floor, the bottom half of the freezer, the washing machine, the clothes dryer, and my work bench—everything—had an atomized coating of blood spatter on it. A casual observer might have concluded my cellar was a place where I regularly slaughtered pigs with dull implements.

The milk of human kindness instantly went sour. Amy got a much less gentle second wash, and an ample amount of adhesive tape in the rebandaging of her ear.

But that's not the end of the story. With one ear taped over, she had trouble with directional hearing, and for the next week of hunting we had a great many "discussions" about our differences of opinion regarding her range.

Then, when the adhesive tape started to shrink a bit, I noticed Amy's eyes seemed to be open very, very wide. It became an expression she wore. Until I retaped the bandage, there was nothing in the world that she resembled quite so much as a dog that had been electrocuted and lived.

Ear ends and the tail tips can be among the most troublesome of injuries—troublesome because there is really no acceptable way to bandage the injury. The cuts are usually tiny and, other than the mess they create, not usually cause for concern. But because they never really get a chance to heal properly, they continue to re-open, and might still be bleeding a month or two after the initial injury. Many setters and pointers hunt the entire season with "pink" tails and ears. Since the incident with Amy, I've been carrying a styptic pencil. It helps to induce clotting in minor cuts, and has become part of my doggie-repair-and-first-aid kit.

The kit contains the following:

- An aerosol can of veterinary "spray bandage," which puts a skinlike film over minor cuts;
- A handful of gauze pads;
- A roll of waterproof adhesive tape;
- A small bottle of hydrogen peroxide;
- A pair of Kelleys (in memory of Duffy);
- A styptic pencil;

- An old Ace bandage;
- A book of paper matches and some Visine eye drops, for minor eye problems;
- Dog toenail clippers;
- A piece of surgical tubing, just in case (God forbid) I ever need a tourniquet;
- A single dog boot;
- A dog comb and a pair of scissors for removing particularly tangled burs from the dog's fur;
- A spare collar and bell;
- A small jar of Vaseline for snow hunting;
- A spray bottle of flea and tick killer.

Everything fits into a Crown Royal sack. Occasionally something major comes up, but as long as I have that collection of stuff back at the truck, most minor dog emergencies can be treated, repaired, patched, or solved, and I can keep hunting. While I will admit to having left home without an American Express card, I've never gone on a day afield without my purple velvet doggie bag.

I was having my teeth cleaned by a very pretty and very pregnant hygienist. She was bubbly and full of conversation until I mentioned that I had been using a scaler just the day before.

"You have a dental scaler at home?" she asked.

I held up two fingers.

"What do you do with them?"

"I clean my dogs' teeth."

Maybe it was the fact that she had her whole hand inside my mouth, but I wasn't speaking too clearly. She heard me say "daughters" when I had said "dogs." Looking back, I can see I should have been tipped off that something was wrong, because she looked at me like I had just mentioned that I had a fetish for pregnant women. There was a long pause before she asked, "You clean their teeth *yourself?*"

"Sure."

"How old are they?"

"Hazel is nine, and Amy is three."

"Why don't you bring them in here?"

"Ha. You'd really go for that, I'll bet."

"Sure, why not."

Nice girl, I thought, but not too many smarts. "It's not a big problem to do it at home. Really. I even brush their teeth for them, so they're used to me poking around in their mouths."

"You brush their teeth for them?"

"Sure."

"How often?"

"About once a month."

She said nothing, so I continued to babble.

"I sit on the cellar floor, put their head on my lap, and go at it. I even use toothpaste."

Another long pause. Finally, "You're serious, aren't you."

I thought I was. "What's wrong?"

She had moved around to the other side of the chair by now, and had the equipment stand between us. "Well, I don't like the way you're treating those girls."

"Wait a minute. Who are we talking about here?"

"Your daughters, Hazel and Amy."

At that instant, if I were a cartoon character, a little light bulb would have gone on over my head. I pondered an appropriate response. There is sometimes a fine line between humor and cruelty, and I'm not entirely sure that I didn't cross it. I tried to keep a straight face. I even squinted my eyes. "They behave like dogs," I said, "so they get treated like dogs."

Gum disease is usually caused by bad teeth. Because of the bacteria that gum disease and bad teeth generate, it is directly linked to kidney failure. And kidney failure, it turns out, is the leading cause of death in dogs that die of "natural causes."

To help your dog live a long and healthy life, keep his teeth clean. I do it myself, but I'm weird. A complete cleaning once every few years by the vet is about right. Oh, I've heard the ads for dog food and biscuits that are supposed to help keep a dog's teeth clean. At best, they only help; they don't do the whole job. What the hell, I brush my own teeth twice a day and that "helps," but every year the hygienist chews me out for not flossing more often. (I think she's still trying to get even.)

Seven human years are equivalent to one dog year, or so we've all heard. I tend to go with an alternative system: If the dog is sexually mature at two, then he's twenty-one. Give him five years for every year thereafter, so that a three-year-old dog is twenty-six, a four-year-old dog is thirty-one, and so on. I've forgotten where I read it, but it's a system that seems to make sense, especially when applied to very young and very old dogs. I was still hunting with Hazel when she was ten. She was past her prime and had hearing problems, but was still doing an acceptable job. Sixty-one seemed more realistic an age equivalent than seventy.

Some old dogs go blind. Mine all seem to go deaf. Unfortunately, it does not always occur at the very end of their lifetimes, and they spend their last several seasons unable to hear my whistle. I'm not convinced that firing a shotgun over a dog's head several hun-dred times each fall doesn't damage his hearing. But I've talked to veterinarians about the problem, with the idea of finding something that could prevent it, and they tell me other dogs who never hear more than an occasional firecracker on the Fourth of July end up going deaf at about the same age. The consensus seems to be that dogs just plain wear out, and not always evenly. In the wild, a dog lives long enough to reproduce, and after that old Mother Nature pretty much forgets about him.

The good news is that in the world of dogs, the primary sense organ is neither eyes nor ears, but nose, and that faculty seems to be that last to go. Just so long as Ol' Sparky retains his scenting ability, the impact of a hearing loss is not as serious as it would be for a human. A dog that is blind or deaf gets along much better than we humans would with a similar loss. The bad news is that losses in hearing or eyesight will keep an otherwise physically sound older hunting dog out of the field during gunning season.

If nothing else, eventually a dog's physical stamina diminishes to a point that it begins to effect the way he hunts. With most dogs, that begins around their seventh year. At that stage of his career, Ol' Sparky doesn't cover his ground as well and certainly can't last as long as he did just two years earlier, but his bird sense keeps his overall effectiveness viable. He's over the hill, but he still has a long way to go before he reaches the bottom.

Appreciating an older dog is a unique pleasure—something that a man with a kennelfull of bird dogs can't take time to experience. If you're lucky—and luck is indeed the biggest factor in it—you can continue to enjoy your dog through his declining years; that is, three or four seasons, or if you're very lucky, five. But the sad truth is that an athletic bird dog really can work himself to death, and it is not unusual for a dog that has been hunted hard all his life to suffer a very sharp decline once he is past his peak.

The short, yelping cries from the cellar seemed to die away, then begin anew a moment later. The puppy had been whining incessantly for the past half-hour. Susan shifted irritably in her chair, then folded her cribbage hand in exasperation. "That whimpering is driving me crazy."

"Bad cards, huh?" I tried not to smile.

"It's not bothering you?"

I shrugged.

After a moment, Susan glanced at her cards again, but in the background the yowling took on a new, higher pitch. She closed her eyes. "Isn't there something you can do to keep that little dog quiet?"

The answer, of course, was "no," especially since I held a triple run of three and had slipped a pair of jacks into the crib, but I got up and went into the cellar anyway.

In her temporary pen, puppy Zelda ran to the wire screen and jumped with glee at the sight of me. She would have done the same if the son of Frankenstein had come down the stairs. This was her first night away from her litter mates, and she had a bad case of the lonelies. An alarm clock ticking beneath a hot water bottle in her nest box—tips from Tap that may have worked for him, but tonight Zelda wasn't having any truck with them; she was alone, and she knew it. I sat on the stairs and watched as the pup alternately stood on her hind legs and frantically clawed at the wire in my direction, then retreated and sat on the newspapers, crying all the while.

Being penned-in isn't fun. Outside, a late-January snowstorm whistled under the eves. There are times when I can feel very much a prisoner in my own house. So I leaned into Zelda's pen and picked her up (five pounds of instantly happy English setter) and sat with her for a moment. When she attacked my fingers with puppy-sharp teeth, I squeezed her muzzle and told her "No!" and put her back in the little enclosure. She immediately went back to whining.

On the other side of the cellar my old Brittany slept snugly. Deaf as a stone, she hadn't even heard me come down the stairs. In years past, Winnie had been my number-one bird dog, but her last season was behind her. In a moment of inspiration I went to her and carried her into Zelda's pen. She wasn't happy about it. But what the hell, I told myself, she's deaf. The puppy's whining isn't going to bother her. And maybe things will work out.

I watched the two dogs long enough to be sure Winnie wasn't going to snap at the puppy, but I knew she wouldn't (my old Brit was to gentle what Babe Ruth was to home run). Zelda nipped at Winnie's legs a few times in a "play with me" invitation, but Winnie stoically ignored her and lay down in the nest box. The puppy nuzzled Winnie's belly, vainly searching for a teat the old spayed Brittany didn't have, then, after another try at the "let's play" routine, she curled up next to Winnie.

When I returned to the fireplace and the cribbage game, Susan was listening to the silence. She was smiling. "What'd you do?"

"I took my cards with me. I knew you'd look at my hand."

"No, I mean with the puppy—she's quiet."

"I put Winnie in the pen with her. Motherhood wins again."

Susan looked at me to be sure I wasn't joking, then announced, "I've got to see this."

We crept down the cellar stairs together and peeked around the corner. Winnie peered out at us, puzzled and somewhat resigned, certain she was being punished once more for something she didn't understand. Eight months later both Winnie and the puppy who now slept against her furry warmth would be dead—one by euthanasia, the other the victim of a passing car—but tonight Winnie was not quite voluntarily acting out the last useful task of a life that had, since its beginning, had me at its center. I tried, but no matter how much I read into her expression that evening or any of the other nights of the next month she slept in the puppy's pen, I never saw anything that resembled maternal contentment. I smiled back at Winnie's sad eyes.

Someone who was not a friend once told me that you ruin your first few bird dogs, then for the rest of your life you never again have a dog as good as those first ones. I still don't like that guy, and it irks me to think he was close to being right. Most of what I learned in training Winnie had to do with how not to handle a sensitive bird dog. Her predecessor had been an intense, supercharged dog. So, of course, I always compared gentle Winnie unfavorably and managed to overlook her positive traits. She was the absolute best retriever of crippled birds I've ever seen anywhere, and although her motor always seemed in need of hotter spark plugs, it was that nonhysterical quality that made her so deadly on woodcock.

That was Winnie, of whom I've written so much; she's left a scar on my heart that still hasn't completely healed. On the cellar stairs that snowy evening, I faced again the question that every hunter who picks out a pup from a litter has to ponder sooner or later: What do you do with a washed-up bird dog, one who can't hunt any longer, one who old age has gotten in a strangle-hold, one who has no future? Whatever decision you arrive at, none are easy— not even the decision to make no decision. Old dogs don't just fade away, no matter how you might wish otherwise. Farmers (at least the ones I know) make it a point not to give names to their animals. Pets can become hazardous to your emotional health, especially at parting time.

And an old bird dog can tear your heart out.

Although I'm a sucker for dog stories, I don't like the gimmick of personifying dogs. The only time, it seems, that dogs are noteworthy is when they act like humans, so it follows that Lassie and Rin Tin Tin fostered a generation of imitators that seem to be honest, sincere people trapped inside a dog's body.

Too bad.

I like dogs because they're *not* people. Sure, I know they can exhibit human traits. And maybe Lassie earned her keep by rescuing Timmy a few times each month. But me, I want my dogs to bark when someone rings the doorbell. Give me *dog* dogs that like to dig holes and fetch things and roll in cow flops. And, forgive me this one vanity, I want them to behave like dogs and go berserk when I put on my hunting clothes.

And Winnie, for whatever else she might or might not have been, was at least a *dog* dog.

A dozen years later, even from this distance, it still seems like the sort of thing that belongs in someone else's story. In the last months of her life, Winnie permitted us to sleep nights by being, if not exactly a mother, at least a mommy to Zelda. In return, I indulged in one of Winnie's lifelong fantasies. I took her rabbit hunting.

It was another what-the-hell decision. She had been pointing rabbits all her life, anyway. Bird dogs, of course, are supposed to ignore furry game. Winnie had never completely agreed with that edict, and whenever I saw her break out of her easy-going hunting style and into a run, it was safe to assume she had started a bunny. I would holler at her, and she would come slinking back, looking guilty, but never quite so remorseful that she could resist the temptation to pretend that she was a beagle when next she smelled the redolence of hasenpfeffer on the hoof.

Rabbit season ran through the end of February. She could only last for an hour or so, but we went out nearly every day the weather permitted. She'd yelp softly, almost to herself, when a rabbit would run from one of her points, and Winnie's aging legs would sprint again, if only for a dozen steps.

It was a good year for rabbits, if not for bird dogs. Near the end, she even stopped looking guilty.

Dogs just show you where the birds are.
They don't hypnotize them.

Havaliah Babcock

seven

That's Why
They Call It
Hunting

It starts sometime in December. One of the local businesses passes out calendars. You flip through the year and come to the month with the picture that's so perfect it's almost a cliché: an incredibly blue sky, a stone wall, an English setter, and the inevitable sugar maple in all its autumn glory.

An artistic person might call the photo "evocative," but if you're a bird hunter it has a terrible beauty that causes a tightening in the pit of your stomach and makes you take a quick breath. The feeling is like the mild shock you get when you catch yourself just as you start to fall. It's an adrenaline rush—and more. For want of a better term I call it The Thump.

Cleaning the cellar in February, you accidentally knock a boot to the floor, and as you replace it The Thump hits you again. It's an involuntary reflex, like the drool from Pavlov's dogs. You feel the worn laces and scarred leather and your body automatically assumes it's going hunting.

As long as you're paying attention, the little reminders can't affect you. It's only when they sneak up on you that The Thump can bowl you over in an emotional landslide.

While in traffic, some change falls under the seat. When you try to blindly fish it out you discover a 20-gauge shell that has been hiding in the darkness for months, waiting to hit you with The Thump. At the theater, you discover a few sticktights on your good pants where they've hung in the closet too close to your hunting jacket. Or, you're in a gallery and you stare at an old Arthur Frost lithograph until you're actually in the woods behind two classic setters. Then, as you turn away from the picture, you shiver as The Thump hits you again. Like a half-forgotten photo of an old girlfriend, it does something to you, something vague and disturbing.

But you like it.

Years ago, I wrote a story called "Brown Feathers From My Game Vest." On surface, it dealt with the memories of a hunting season. Looking back, I now realize it was about The Thump. On another occasion I wrote a line in an essay that asked, "Do I love this season because I hunt, or do I love hunting as fervently as I do because it takes place in autumn?" Nobody ever made a big deal over it, but to me it has become the most significant line I've written. If you hunt with a bird dog, you know my meaning; there's no need to explain further.

My wife regularly accuses me of living for the sake of hunting. I no longer argue with her. Her accusation is much too close to the truth to be brushed off with a one-liner. I've heard other people talk of their love or obsession for this or that. Yet when I see their passion held up for comparison, I believe it's nothing next to the love I have for autumn.

Sometimes I wake up in the middle of the night after dreaming November has somehow caught me unprepared, that the bird season is already nearly over but I haven't had the dogs out of the kennel. In the dream, it seemed plausible. I have trouble getting back to sleep, wondering if it was a premonition of something I should be paying attention to.

The coming autumn is a reality, differing only from the last one in how you perceive it—the one fading as the other comes into focus. When you've hunted through nearly a half century of autumns, the next one is a joyous reality already waiting in the future, somehow reaching back to the present, tugging the bird hunter forward. You feel the tug.

In late summer the leaves become darker and duller and the wind blowing through the trees rattles more than whispers. The dogs pace and bark for no reason. Everything is going fine until you glance out the car window and catch sight of an unexpected clump of sumac that has put on its autumn war paint six weeks early. You feel a familiar tightening in the base of your throat.

In other parts of the country hunters can hold The Thump at bay with sorties for early teal or flighting doves. Not so in New England, where August and September can seem to stretch on forever. You reload shells and hit golf balls, all the while trying not to think about the excitement brewing just below the surface. Like claustrophobia, you cannot allow yourself to succumb to it.

Then, quite suddenly, it's here, and there are no longer enough hours in the day. Autumn! We spend the rest of the year waiting for it and talking about it and (in my own case) writing about it, mostly because of something that can only be defined metaphorically: for a few short weeks, every day brings the same thrill that you felt as a ten-year-old kid coming down the stairs on Christmas morning and making that right-hand turn into the living room. There are quivering points and fast shots in the calendar pictures, and gray feathers floating among glowing aspens, and never a need to wish upon a star: you're living out the wish you'd be making.

Like a favorite song you've waited all day to hear on the radio, when it finally plays it's over much too quickly and you're left humming the few snatches of melody you remember. You clean out your hunting gear from the car, and search under the seat for stray shells. The scarred leather boots are put back up in the cellar rafters. Hunting season is over.

It is a bleak time.

But thankfully, our measurements of time are invariably more convenient than conclusive. Just when it seems the autumn you waited so long for has disappeared, you stop at the dry cleaner. The girl behind the counter wishes you a happy holiday season and gives you…a calendar.

It begins again. Can it be that your hands are shaking as you flip past the months? February … April … July … October!

The rain continues, more a steady drizzle than a downpour. We're in the old orchard when Winnie points, then tiptoes ahead when I approach her. I have grouse on my mind and react too quickly when a woodcock takes wing beyond the next apple tree. Two fruitless shots, then I put the empties in my pocket, accept the dog's comments, and put my shooting glasses back into their case. They are now beaded with water and are more hindrance than help. A miss like that one needs an excuse, and "obscured vision" is as good as any.

Within a hundred yards Win points again. An observer taking notes might perceive that I cut much closer to the dog when I think she's pointing a woodcock than I do when there's a chance she might have a grouse. She holds as I do my woodcock walk, but no bird gets up. I glance back at her, and she is looking off to her left. I move there. No bird. Now she is looking further to her left, almost behind her. I move there, and two woodcock spring up, pretending to be fast—my annual chance at a double. I take the far bird cleanly, then pivot to try for the second bird back over my head. I fail to hold under him and miss.

Win brings in the fallen bird, and I scratch her behind a wet ear. I ask if she scented the birds moving or merely spotted them sulking away from my approach, but she just smiles her open-mouthed dog's smile and won't tell.

In my part of the world, woodcock hunting is exactly what it should be. The little patches of cover just outside of town are what sportsmen the world over conjure up when they dream of a woodcock hunting trip, and the suburban New England hunter can make of the game whatever he cares to and not have to pretend anything. A man doesn't have to go to Nova Scotia or Cape May for the world's best woodcock hunting. It's probably right there at the end of his street.

In woodcock hunting, a pointing dog is a necessity. If you want more than just a chance flush or two, don't leave home without one. Having said that, I'm pleased to report that it is one of the very few happy coincidences of the sporting world that a dog needn't be a champion to do an acceptable job on woodcock. The birds are strongly scented and hold so well for a point that the finer things expected in a grouse or a quail dog are luxury options on the basic utility woodcocking model. In fact, sometimes woodcock allow a bird dog to crowd too close, spoiling the dog for more jumpy game birds.

But I love woodcock. They have many predictable habits, chief among which is their ability to charm everyone who has anything to do with them, including hunters.

It is popular in certain circles to accuse eastern woodcock hunters of snobbery: side-by-side doubles, classic dogs, tweeds, gentlemanly rules, and all that. I shoot an over-under and don't own anything tweedy other than my duck hunting hat, but there have been times when I've had to plead guilty as charged. I once met a man, however, who was quite the opposite type. He said to me, "I'd love to go to Africa and shoot one of everything." He was all that any sensible person despises about hunters. Significantly, he also said he wouldn't waste a shell on a woodcock. I'm usually polite, but I think I said "Good."

If a gaudy trophy of a bird strutting by the roadside can bring out the unsportsmanlike worst in some hunters, then woodcock, which are hardly trophies and rank considerably below chickens as table fare, can bring out the very best. Woodcock hunting, after all, is pure fun. Success in the October woodlands is measured in terms of the enjoyment the hunter derives from a day afield with his dog. In this case, the secret to this particular success lies in the fine art of not taking yourself seriously.

It seems a perverse human trait that, at times, we are able to derive enjoyment from our own failings. Woodcocking will do that to a man. There is a hunter inside all of us, a hunter who takes pride in his shooting and knows that 'doodles are so easy we should never miss one. Each time we are "woodcocked" into poking a couple of holes in the sky, the hunter part of us is disgusted. Ah, but the other part of us—the human that offsets the hunter inside—throws his head back and laughs.

Writing about pointing dogs without mentioning hunting is tough, sort of like trying to write about stalactites without mentioning stalagmites. Oh, I know there are men—field trialers—who love and train bird dogs but have never fired a shotgun. Bird dog competition is fine sport, and so long as I'm not spending more than I can afford I enjoy it as much as anyone. But every bird dog deserves a hunter for an owner, even if that owner is a lousy shot. Hunting is what it's all about.

Can what we humans do be legitimately termed hunting? It's a bit of a stretch. Oh, man *thinks* he's hunting, but in truth he's just out for a walk. Dogs hunt. Men give them a ride to the covert, then do a little shooting when the time comes. Afterwards, they carry the dead birds around. But it's the dogs that do the hunting.

Men may have had hunting in their makeup back in some prehistoric era, but we have long since traded that gene for the one that makes us prefer pointing dogs to Siamese cats. Our dogs, by one definition, are four-legged extensions of our lost hunting instincts. (Without being a snob about it, I think a case can be made for the idea that hunting without a dog isn't hunting at all—it's just shooting. In my part of the world, men successfully hunt grouse by the stomp-'em-up-yourself method. Some men even like it. But I'd rather swallow a hammer.) When you have a bird dog along to point, you happen to the bird rather than the bird happening to you. That's hunting.

You know where the birds are. You drive to a place where you've hunted before, knowing full well that the birds are there. But actually finding them is a different story. Here's where the dog comes in. He sees to the scouting, plays the wind, handles the tactical maneuvers, and when he points, it's just as you planned it. In life, there are a few other thrills (a few, but not many) in the same catagory as having lost track of your dog and then finding him on point, standing with his eyes bulging, waiting for you to appear on the scene.

My partner whistled. On the opposite edge of the cut milo I could see his florescent orange hat. Well ahead of him, facing into the prairie breeze, his wirehair stood on point. I put Stella at heel and made a beeline across the field.

As I got close I said, "Stella, hut," and left her standing behind me. A direction was indicated. We would walk in this way and attempt to push the covey that way.

Novice quail hunters are told, "You'll get confused by all the birds in the air. Don't flock shoot. Pick out just one." Maybe it's because I've heard it so much, but I never had a problem that way. Where I *do* have problems is when the covey doesn't go up all at once, but rather, flushes like this one did; they went off like a string of Chinese firecrackers—one, then two, then two more, then three, then a single, then two more. Just as I'd be pulling on one, another bird would distract me. Then, just as I was ready to follow through on that one, still another would distract me. My greatest fear is that I'll end up with two unfired shells in the chambers as the covey sails out of sight.

Not that time. The scattered birds all seemed to be flushing in front of my partner and heading toward the wood edge on his side, but one took the high road and swerved across in front of me, and I put him down with a paint-brush-type swing-through shot.

Then, after the flurry, nothing. My partner started to say something—his wirehair was running after the bird he had dropped—when the last bird went out immediately in front of me. It was a lay-up: an easy right quartering chance. After the shots I opened the gun and caught the pair of empties.

"Did you get him?"

"I threw him back," was all I had to say. There's something about those below-eye-level shots that I can't seem to master.

I turned around and waved to Stella. After all that, she was still standing where I had left her. She came up and it took her only a few moments to find the bob I had dropped.

Then, as always, the post-covey question: "Did you follow them?"

"I had them heading into the woods on your side."

"Naw. I saw a couple turn left out beyond those tall weeds."

If the truth be known, neither of us had given the flight of the covey our undivided attention, thereby compounding our stupidity by a factor of two. Frank Roach, a dog pro from the Texas Panhandle, originally taught me what little I know about quail hunting. He used to sit on his horse and yell at me, "Let the dogs worry about finding those birds. Your job is to watch the covey." It's one of those things that's easier said than done. For thirty years in New England I've been taking my birds one at a time, and I'm stuck in a rut that won't let me ignore a bird I've hit.

We started off in the general direction that the covey had taken. Sometimes, but not often, they'll set in as a compact group. This bunch was scattered when they took off, so that seemed unlikely. In a weed belt Stella pointed. We walked in but nothing developed. When I sent her ahead, she crept forward and then, gradually, lost the scent entirely and began hunting again. The wirehair was more methodical, and where Stella gave up she pointed, looking nearly straight down into the grass.

My partner kicked the bird out—another below-eye-level opportunity, thankfully on his side. Twenty minutes later, after a thorough search, that was the only single we could find. If fifteen birds originally flushed and we only took two, the singles had to be somewhere. We just couldn't find them. Maybe they tucked themselves deep in the thick stuff. Maybe they were air-washed more than woodcock or pheasants.

But, more likely, maybe we should have done a better job of watching where they set in.

It is difficult for me to be completely objective about quail. Maybe if I lived in quail country and hunted them all through the autumn and into the winter I could say something that sounded like wisdom, but I don't and I can't. If you have a question for me about quail hunting, write it down and hide it in a safe place.

There aren't any quail in New England. (Oh, there are a few on Cape Cod—I even wrote a story about hunting them there—but lately the Cape has become wall-to-wall houses. Among the few certainties in life is the fact that the best coverts always make ideal building lots.) So for reasons I don't fully understand, when things close down in New England after the first of the year, I put my dogs in crates and drive half way across the country to hunt quail.

Some bird dogs are specialists. Thankfully, most seem to be general practitioners with something of the appliance in their makeup: plug them in anywhere and they operate on full current. When called upon, each of my New England grouse dogs has done a workmanlike job on coveys and, although not consistently, on singles, too. And I know there's a quail-specific learning process, because each one gets better each year.

If shooting quail was all I was interested in, I'd leave the dogs back home and hire a guide. But I'm a bird dog guy. One thing I will never do again is pay money to hunt with someone else's dogs; if you take pride in your dogs, you shouldn't, either. The only real prerequisites for quail hunting with nonquail specialists are that your dogs stop when you tell them to and hold a point while you and your partner get into position, which can sometimes take a few minutes. They'll find birds.

In quail hunting there are problems—but there are solutions, too. In some parts of the country you have to boot your dogs to protect their feet from cacti and ground spurs. Universally, dogs act like they're wearing snowshoes when you first tape boots on them. That lasts until the breakaway whistle. Then, almost immediately, it's hunting as usual.

My setters pick up cockleburs, but I rub Vaseline in their armpits and it helps. Trimming their feathering to nearly nothing helps, too. But it's not an accident that pointers and German shorthairs are the prevalent breeds in quail country.

More than pheasants in the edges, more than grouse in old orchards, or woodcock beneath popple canopies, quail hunting demands that a hunter and his dogs play the wind. Bird dogs figure it out quickly enough, but I'm just a mongrel with an indifferent nose and it took me longer than it should have. My excuse was that I was from New England. Not that we don't have wind, but it's just not often a consideration in the woods and in thick stuff.

By themselves, covey flushes are enough to keep any man who loves shooting coming back for more. Factor into the formula the wonderfully lucid dog work quail provide and the idea that a hunter can keep his dog "in birds" for a comparatively large percentage of the time. Finally, add in the quail themselves—in front of the dog, on the wing, on the plate—like a dream, they're all you hope they'll be.

But even all that doesn't explain driving halfway across the country in January. My wife is sure I'm crazy. The catalyst in the equation (or maybe it's an extraneous root) is the pointing addiction.

When I was a kid, my father was a Saturday hunter. In my early teens, before I became overly interested in football and girls, I used to go hunting with my dad on autumn Saturday mornings. Although the game laws required a hunter to be sixteen, minors of at least fourteen were permitted to hunt on the same license (and bag limit) as an accompanying adult. That is, if the kid could persuade the adult to let him take a turn. I started working on Dad as soon as I turned fourteen.

We owned a succession of indifferent orange-and-white Brittany spaniels back then, each of which was named "Freckles." (Thirty-five years later, it is difficult to remember where one dog stopped and the next began. From this distance, all are referred to as "One of the Freckleses.")

Now, Dad was the sort of man who assumed that when the time came, the kids would do okay. Since I was one of the kids, it shouldn't have surprised me that his assumptions applied to me, too. So one Saturday morning he handed me Old Betsy. "Carry this for a while. Keep the dog with you," was all he said. Then, as was his wont, he left me alone and went to walk with his hunting partner.

My turn had come.

A word here about Old Betsy. Everybody owns an old gun they refer to by that name. This one was a hump-backed Remington Model 11. She was long and heavy—nearly ten pounds when loaded—and had a classic double-shuffle recoil that, once you got used to it, was not unpleasant. Like other well-used tools, Betsy had taken on the character of her user: the checkering was worn smooth and the receiver had the silvered patina that only comes through years of handling. The safety was a troublesome miniature second trigger that had to be pushed forward before the gun could be fired—all but impossible to do with cold fingers. That old gun was a challenge to take apart and a nightmare to put back together, but all the internals had the unassuming beauty of well-machined steel.

For nearly all of Dad's life, Old Betsy was his one-and-only gun. Ducks and pheasants were always his main quarry, but an occasional partridge and even a few wood-cock were centered—and as often as not, blown to smithereens—by a choke that contrived to put all the pel-lets into the very center of a thirty-inch circle at forty yards.

By the time that Saturday morning in 1961 arrived, I had shot that gun enough so that it was no longer the mystery it once was. But shooting was one thing, and car-rying a gun was something else. Although I had often imagined the moment when Dad would hand me the gun, I hadn't planned on the handicap that an unwieldy ten-pound hunk of artillery could represent. It was a lot like shouldering a fully loaded haversack: suddenly the very act of walking required some skill and planning.

After a while, one of the Freckleses scared up a pheas-ant, and my first shot was at hand. I was cool.

Shoot for the head, because pheasants in flight are half tailfeathers. I knew that. It was something I had been told a hundred times. So, of course, I proceeded to shoot the bird's tail off with my first shot. The rooster flew on with his nearly naked fanny hanging down, held aloft by a temporary restraining order against the laws of physics. It never occurred to me to shoot a second time.

I was, as I said earlier, cool.

The bird crossed over a little rise and finally fell, more from faulty aerodynamics than any fatal damage my shooting might have done. I hurried one of the Freckleses over to where the bird had fallen and arrived just in time to see a beagle pull my pheasant from under a brush pile.

"Hey, that's my bird." I hollered, but the beagle wasn't having any truck with that. He was going to get the pheasant to his owner, and he was sure I wasn't him. I made a try at catching with the dog. I still had arches and could run pretty well in those days, and in my mind I could see the headlines: "Fleeing Beagle Caught by Young Nimrod— Historic First Pheasant Recovered."

Unfortunately, my own headline ultimately read, "Beagle Absconds with Pheasant: Outruns Kid Carrying Ten-Pound Anti-Tank Gun—Only Tailfeathers Salvaged."

Good dogs handle game birds, no matter what type of feathers they might wear. Released pheasants aren't tough, but it is a rare bird dog that can consistently point a pheasant of the see-you-later native variety. The rarest thing in pheasant hunting is that which is also the most popular scene with outdoor artists—the spectacular flush of a rooster that is being pointed in the open. In the late 1960s, the Crystals had a popular song that explained it all. Loosely paraphrased it went, "They do run run run, they do run run."

Hens are legal wherever the Fish & Game folks have given up on the idea of creating a self-sustaining pheasant population. Any pheasant hunter with a pointing dog will prefer, if he stops to think about it, hens to cocks; hens tend to be quicker and better fliers than roosters, and they sit tight when roosters run. Not always, to be sure, but often enough so that, whenever I'm in the pay-for-play game, I ask that all hens be put out.

In truth, if I were exclusively a pheasant hunter, I might own a springer spaniel. Springers are easy to like, and seem ideally suited to a bird who puts more trust in the infantry than the air force.

Yes, I like springers. But you see, I have this pointing addiction...

William Harden Foster authored *New England Grouse Shooting*. As such, he is broadly credited with being one of the founding fathers of what we know of as modern grouse hunting. Recognized as an expert, he is frequently quoted on semantical questions. Something that has always tickled me is that he shot *only at grouse his dog pointed*—at least in his books he did. I suspect that in the field he was pretty much like you and me and took his shots as they came.

I say that because he is further credited with originating the game of skeet, which he introduced as a practice for actual grouse shooting. His game of skeet, of course, consists of crossing shots, overhead shots, and even a few that might be the sort a hunter might get over a dog on point.

Very few.

You are welcome to draw your own conclusions about the founders of modern grouse hunting, but if skeet shooting indicated the way they went about it, I think shots over solid points were the exception rather than the rule back then, just as they are today.

Grouse hunting is more than just bird shooting with trees. The bird is smart like a burglar alarm is smart. Even on a good day, he's jumpy. Success requires all the dog has got, and even then points sometimes fall easily into three catagories:

Type A, the *walking point*, is when the grouse refuses to cooperate and hold still.

Type B is the *spring-loaded point*, which is that knife-edge balancing act that hangs in equilibrium so long as neither hunter nor dog moves.

Type C is the *pinned-down point*, which casts doubt upon Havaliah Babcock's contention that the dog does not hypnotize the bird. If I ever get to heaven, I'll let you know if my suspicions are right: heaven, I think, must be a place where you regularly get three or four grouse points of the type-C variety in a day's hunt.

Certainly, going after any bird in its own element tilts the scales in its favor, but when the bird is the professionally nervous ruffed grouse, a dog charged with pinning the bird regularly needs something extraordinary. The unfortunate part of the equation is that right around the time a bird dog finally figures out how to do it right, he dies of old age. My own best grouse dog, in her best year, recorded eighty grouse points. There are grouse dogs that are better than Hazel was in 1984. I know they exist because people tell me about them. I've just never seen one.

In the rain, what's left of the grimy snowbank has the rotted look of a sponge that has seen its last car wash. The pebbles and dirt that the plow had thrown up along with the snow are now exposed in the receding mass. The stuff can hardly be called snow any longer except in those places where the undercut bank has fallen in on itself, revealing its almost-white interior. The right fender of the truck nudges the bank as I pull onto the shoulder. Hazel pops her head up and peers out the window at the Bondsville covert across the street. Her tail wags and the bell on her collar tinkles rhythmically. She knows.

I shut off the wipers and ignition, then sit for a minute scratching Hazel's ears and watching the rain distort my view through the windshield. The scene beyond, although a typical picture of December in New England, is hardly a Christmas-card setting. Pneumonia weather, my mother used to call it. *Only a fool would be out hunting on a day like this.* I grin. On the seat next to me is my fool's hunting jacket. I'm already wearing my fool's hat and my fool's rubber bib-fronts.

With the open gun in the crook of my arm, we start across the street and into the covert. "Miss Hazelberry," I call, "you've got a fool for a master." She stops and looks back at me for a moment, then casts ahead and crosses the stream to my right. She has sewn up the primary qualification for a good hunting companion: she keeps her opinions to herself.

I approach the brook crossing, wondering how much deeper than usual it will be with the rain and melting snow we've had. From the tangle of willows immediately on the other side a grouse erupts, banking over the line of bushes to quickly drop out of sight beyond. Moments later, I see him climb away from the stream course and head for the shelter of the tall pine woods beyond the swamp. Dumbfounded, I look down at the still-empty chambers of my open gun, then back at the truck two hundred feet behind me. Things aren't supposed to happen this way. I shake my head, and take out a pair of shells from the pocket of my rain jacket.

Once across the stream, my thinking changes. It is just as well, I assure myself. What kind of story would that have made, anyway? *I got out of the truck and walked into the woods. A grouse flew up, so I shot him. It was raining. I went home. The end.*

Hazel checks in, and I wave her into the willows. She is already wet, and her skin shows pink through her setter's coat. She locates the bird scent along the brook, and won't leave it until I walk on. "Come on, bird brain. He's already left." Finally, she races ahead.

In the open fields to our right the rain is being blown down in sheets, but beneath the trees it's relatively calm.

During the previous week I hunted in the snow with icicles forming on my mustache. The thaw began yesterday. Although the temperature hovers just above freezing, today's emphasis will be on staying dry rather than warm. I generate plenty of heat inside my waterproofs, just so long as I'm not wet.

The bib-fronts are rubber coated, but my brand-new hat and jacket are of a "breathable" material that is guaranteed waterproof. I harbor my doubts. Clothing flexes as it's worn, and the continual brushing of rain-laden branches against the jacket will be the ultimate test.

We cross an arm of the swamp that defines the edge of the covert. Shelves of ice persist underfoot, unseen beneath the sedge grass, almost but not quite strong enough to support my weight. I try to step from one hummock to the next.

If moving quietly were an asset in grouse hunting, then rainy days would be superior to others. It isn't, and they're not. We continue through the covert, hunting along a brook where beavers have thinned the alders and birches. Two months previous, a flight of woodcock spent an October day here, resting from their night's journey. Hazel and I interrupted the afternoon nap of a few of their number. She slashes now through the same brush and beaver paths. I wonder if she remembers?

At the edge of a frozen swamp pond, four black ducks jump at our approach. I hold on the farthest bird as they cross, and when a second, nearer duck joins him in my sight picture, I say, "Bingo—two at once." Why can't I have the presence of mind to do that during duck season instead of blasting holes in the air as fast as I can pull the trigger? The four blacks continue on, climbing as they circle the open area around the pond; then, uncharacteristically, they swing back over me as if to get a good look at the sort of fool who hunts in the rain and passes up sucker shots. The ice on the pond is covered by a layer of rain water, but there is an open spring hole by the near shore. The blacks want to return, but fly on after a moment's indecision.

Black ducks and New England winters seem to go together. They're supposed to be among the smartest of waterfowl, but their habit of remaining through the most bitter months of the year rather than heading south with their supposedly duller cousins does not speak well of their intelligence. Maybe, though, they find something in winter that only they appreciate. I smile at the thought that I may well be a black duck at heart.

Only grouse remain legal game during these closing days of the year. All the other seasons have come and gone. Any stupid birds have either gotten smart or have taken their rightful place on the food chain. The grouse that are left have survived weather extremes and preda-tors of all kinds, including those with shotguns. They're wary. If killing grouse were all that grouse hunting were about, December would be a terrible month for it. My father used to say there isn't enough hunt in hunting to go out just for the sake of hunting alone. He always made a joke of that, perhaps out of a sense of embarrassment over philosophizing. But he was right. The most important item I'll bring home today are the memories that will last through the winter days ahead. I couldn't stay home even if I had to.

In the farthest corner of the covert, where the swamp and timbered land beyond come together, Hazel points. The cover is fairly open, with just a scattering of hemlock shrubs and some low-growing blueberry bushes. When nothing develops from a pass in front of her point I assume that the bird has run ahead, and I whistle her on. She races forward, but strikes scent again fifty yards farther along and slows by degrees until she is stretched out on a low point before a tangle of hemlocks. It seems inevitable:

no matter which side I will go to, the bird will come out the other. Situations like this are best handled the way a pointer puppy handles a bird field. Charge!

As I move into the evergreen thicket, I hear the grouse boil up and think for a moment he has escaped, but then he passes very close by my face on his way out. I dodge and then turn to fire, but he is quickly gone.

I call to Hazel and sit with her for a minute on a rock outcropping. "At least he didn't fly off thinking he had out-smarted us, Haze." She takes no part in my discussion, preferring instead to tell me her troubles, most of which have to do with us sitting rather than moving on. She races ahead when I get to my feet.

We work our way back toward the truck along the opposite side of the covert, where timbering operations a few years back have left an abundance of deadfalls and slash piles. Briars took hold when the forest canopy was cleared, and still persist in thick brakes in each opening. The only positive way to hunt thorns is to have a dog that doesn't give a damn. Hazel qualifies. I skirt the edges, lis-tening to her bell and half hoping it doesn't go silent as she busts through the heart of the thickets.

In a thorn-filled orchard it happens: I can see the tip of her tail where she is pointing beyond some juniper, but as I start toward her she moves forward on a walking point.

Maybe the bird can be headed off by a circling maneu-ver. As I struggle to get into position I find myself mutter-ing my own version of The Grouse Hunter's Prayer. It's not fraught with hosannas and hallelujahs, but is a simple, re-peated, "Just let him stay put until I clear this damn tangle...Just until I get beyond this (Ouch!) thornapple..."

But the bird is no fool, and to keep from being out-flanked he flushes as soon as the covering briar patch runs out. The shot is a left quartering chance with the grouse flying at eye level. The gun comes up easily. The bird fal-ters at my shot, seeming to stand on his tail in midair, then rights himself and continues on. My second shot strikes the bole of a birch tree at a range of six feet. Beyond the cloud of flying splinters and bits of bark I see the grouse curving to the right as he clears a distant apple tree.

Hit in the tail. I shake my head. He may or he may not be carrying pellets. I walk to the birch tree and run my fingers over the finely splintered wound where the load of 7½'s struck. I saw the bird clearly. A better shot with the first barrel wouldn't have left me saying, "If only this tree hadn't jumped into the way..." Why is it that I can regularly hit 90 percent of the targets on the skeet range, yet can easily blow four or five opportunities in a row while hunting? Of course, I'd be among the first to admit that skeet shooting, with both feet firmly planted and nothing but air between gun and target bears as much similarity to actual grouse shooting as paging through a *Playboy* magazine does to taking out a cute divorcee for drinks and dinner.

We hunt along what I guess to be the bird's line of flight, skirting the ridge that borders the cleared land to our left. About the time I am ready to conclude that we should turn around and work back along the opposite side, Hazel stops suddenly in her tracks as she passes a fallen oak tree top. She hardly has time to stop. Almost instantaneously the grouse takes flight from the far side of the deadfall, slanting away downhill. I fire quickly through the screening brush, and although I don't see the bird fall, I feel the shot was "on."

I scramble through the slash, calling to Hazel to follow. Beyond the tangle, a float of feathers hangs in the rain like a three dimensional punctuation mark where shot charge and grouse came together. "Find dead, Hazel— dead bird here." She burrows back into the slash, seemingly crawling on her elbows, and after a moment backs out with the grouse. I look back at the bits of fluff still floating in the air. Why can't every blind shot be as certain as this one?

The bird's feathers are wet, and will be wetter by the time I take him from my gamebag back at the truck. When I staple this grouse tail to the carrier beam in the cellar, I will forever know this bird was taken in the rain: the feathers will never regain their vibrancy.

Hazel waits for the heart and liver as I field dress the bird. This might be the last grouse of the season for me. I've been thinking the same of every bird Hazel has brought to me for the past couple weeks. The Indians used to say a prayer over their fallen game, asking the animal's spirit to forgive the hunter. Instead, I smooth the feathers on the bird's breast, half wishing that, like my fisherman friends, I could release him to fight again on another day.

If there can be a real difference between hunting and simply killing, it must exist in the attitude of those who hunt. Hunting is a game played, by and large, without benefit of referees or a specific set of rules. It is a private, solitary experience, and like other solitary games, the truly important rules are those you make for yourself. What you get out of it is up to you and you alone.

The rain continues. With the bird in the gamepocket of my jacket we start back toward the truck. As we near the road the new-old smell of a coal stove wafts by, all the more pungent in the moist air. Unconsciously, I've stopped hunting and have the gun under my arm rather than at ready, but Hazel races through the cover undeterred.

If man as a species does not need to hunt, some men do, just as some men need to work the soil, or compete, or drive fast cars. I don't pretend any longer that there is a hunter inside each human. Killing for sport has become highly unfashionable, after all. It is a mistake to expect understanding from those ultracivilized folks who simply cannot come to terms with the idea that food was once alive. "If killing game birds was all I got out of the sport, I'd have given it up a long time ago." I've used that Burton Spiller quote so often I've nearly worn it out, but all my arguments seldom had any effect on anyone who believed that, as a hunter, I was only slightly better than a crazed hatchet murderer.

Other people assume that because I kill game birds, I must hate them. That alone is a measure of how shallow their understanding of it all is. Frank Perdue, after all, kills a lot of chickens each day, but I doubt if he hates them. No. I've given up trying to convince people that there really is a human inside each hunter. The one thing I am certain of is that I've nothing to apologize for.

As we approach the truck I take a fast inventory. Thanks to several thousand applications of mink oil, my boots are still nearly dry. And while the hat seems to have lived up to its promise, the shoulders and sleeves of the sweater I've worn under the "waterproof" jacket are soaked. I'll have to break out my old and often-patched nylon/neoprene rain shirt from my war bag if I'm to hunt anymore today.

As I dig out the keys and let Hazel into the truck, I notice that the palms of my hands are shriveled from the rain. Hazel sits on the floor of the cab, already having begun waiting to be let out at the next covert. At this stage of her life she is so good that I worry about her dying young. I look from her to my wrinkled fingerprints, wondering if I might really be a fool.

"You actually *like* to hunt in the rain, don't you?" My wife accused me that morning. I hadn't denied it. "Rain, snow, fog, windy or calm, hot or cold, wet or dry—it doesn't matter," I answered. "I like to hunt. Period. Maybe a tornado would keep me home, or an earthquake...It would have to be a *big* earthquake, you understand." She hadn't thought my reply was at all funny. More than anyone else, she knows how close to the truth even the exaggerations can be.

Fool? Golfers out in the rain are fools, or mountain climbers risking their necks for thrills. Or ice fishermen, sitting around freezing off certain posterior portions of their bodies. But me? Why, New Year's and the end of the grouse season are just a few days away. Then what?·I grin to myself as I get out the war bag from behind the seat. "Miss Hazelberry, what do *you* think?"

Her tail wags with renewed enthusiasm. She knows.

To everything there is a season,
and a time for every purpose
under heaven.

Eccles. 3:1

eight

Life Cycles and the Complete Bird Dog

What is it that changes a puppy into a bird dog? What special interaction of experience and bloodlines and training? For that matter, when can you tell about a pup? Even from the same litter, one dog will turn out to be "just okay" while another will be the kind hunters wish for when they blow out birthday candles. Why?

Earlier, I identified the three components that go into the makeup of every bird dog: breeding, training, and experience. In chapter two, I called these three the "components of greatness." But it seems each of these is further governed by a few specific elements in the dog's makeup.

For want of better terms, I've called them *imprinting,
endurance, trainability, hunting ability* (which I refer to
as "hunt/search"), and *bird sense.* These five elements
seem to ebb and flow in a more-or-less predictable
cyclical fashion.

As obvious as the elements themselves might be, their
individual cycles remain a mystery to most dog owners. So
I've plotted the sequence of these cycles through the lifetime of a typical bird dog.

Understand, this is not high science: no research
grants, no double-blind tests, no quantitative analysis of
reams of data. The chart is based only on my twenty-five
years of observing bird dogs—those I've trained and those
that belonged to my friends. It's hardly accurate. Think of
it in terms of a general strategic battle plan rather than a
specific set of tactical marching orders—it's not meant to
pinpoint anything. There is, after all, no good way to attach quantitative values to something as elusive as a dog's
bird sense or hunting ability.

To everything there is a season. There is one right period for teaching a dog manners, and another for encour-

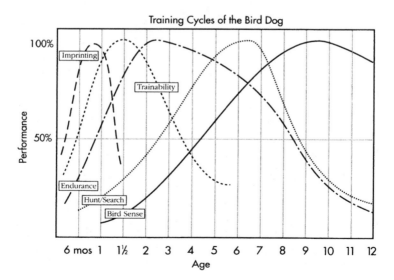

Training Cycles of the Bird Dog

aging him to run. There is a right time to let him chase birds, and another for insisting that he stand steady. And, most importantly, there is a time to correct mistakes, and a time to be tolerant of them. Once the cycle theory is understood, the importance of a harmonious training schedule becomes clear.

The big question in producing a quality bird dog changes from "Which of these elements is the most important?" to "Which is the most important right now, at this particular stage of the dog's development?"

There are going to be a lot of different opinions regarding the concepts expressed in the chart. My opinion is only that of an amateur bird dog trainer, but since I'm the one who made it up, I get to go first:

Imprinting. This is something that happens early in a young dog's life. The things that he's exposed to as a puppy put him on a path that will determine what sort of dog he's *inclined* to become later. For example, a friend of mine had the pick of a litter of setters, and chose a classic-looking female. Unfortunately, he was going through a divorce during the puppy's first year, and had very little time for doggie matters. I don't mean to say that the dog was mistreated, because my friend spent a great deal of money to be sure she was fed and cared for. But the pup just wasn't exposed to much of anything outside the kennel. Now, years later, even though the dog has been with several professional trainers, my friend complains that his dog isn't "birdy" enough.

If the truth be told, she isn't. The two of her litter mates we've kept track of both turned out well, but she became the dog she was inclined to be from her imprinting: shy, unenthusiastic, and difficult to train. Imprinting is going to happen, whether the puppy is positively influenced by bird scent and human contact and the excitement of going afield, or negatively affected by the boredom of days spent inside a kennel waiting for dinner.

When compared to the other factors, imprinting doesn't seem like a big deal. But like some trace element without which life is not possible, it is a basic and highly critical essential in the makeup of any good bird dog. If the dog is to fulfill the promise of his pedigree, there is one right period for positive imprinting, and it cannot be duplicated later no matter how much time is spent with the dog.

Trainability is an elusive element that determines a dog's willingness to be taught things by people. Elusive, because it is a measure not so much of what he knows, but how easily he trains. A casual observer might be impressed with the results of training, but the trait of trainability is hereditary, and unlike its results, it is far less obvious to someone not actually involved in dog training.

But the trainability of a puppy is not the point here. Rather, the trainability cycle shows that time in his life when his receptiveness to training is at its peak. That one best time to train young Sparky will wax and then wane early in his life. He needs the yard work and field training you'll give him before he can ever become a good bird dog, and you've got a relatively short time to teach him what he needs to know. Although not as severely restrictive as imprinting, there is only one right period for training, and trying to make up for lost time later in the dog's life can be an exercise in futility.

Endurance is the one area where just about every hunter knows what he wants: "I don't want a dog that poops out before I do; Sparky has got to outlast *me*."

But for the complete hunting dog, endurance becomes a factor measured in terms of days rather than hours. The graph of a dog's strength development looks a lot more like Prudential's Rock of Gibraltar than a ebb-and-flow cycle, but strength development is a cyclical function nevertheless. Because dogs develop all their stamina during their first couple of seasons, the graph climbs steadily to peak in year two. The dog's endurance remains solid through his prime, then begins a gradual but steady decline until Father Time catches up to him in his tenth or eleventh season. A properly developed bird dog is unimpeded by any lack of physical strength and stamina from the time he is two until well into his sixth year.

Hunt/search is something I earlier defined as all the things that a good bird dog does when he does not have birds. It is a hunting dog spending his energy intelligently. It's a skill that a bird dog teaches himself, one that takes all of his early years to learn. If you've ever hunted behind a quality bird dog late in his prime, you'll know how well developed this ability can become. Like a skilled craftsman, a good bird dog can be a joy to watch—even to the non-sportsman. Hunt/search cycles upward a year or so behind endurance because it is a function that depends on endurance. Likewise, hunt/search will not decline until a dog's endurance drops. At that point, Ol' Sparky knows what he should do, but just doesn't have the stamina to do it any longer.

Bird sense is what separates good, practicing bird dogs from those that might be of the same breeding but ended up, in the puppy lottery, with an owner who hadn't contracted the disease known as the pointing addiction. As I wrote earlier, a bird dog is expected to find a game bird that is trying hard not to be found, then handle it in a manner so that it can be pointed. A dog with bird sense is the fabric of our daydreams; he's what we're all hoping for when we reach down into a box of squirming puppies and pick one out.

Like hunt/search, bird sense is a skill the dog teaches himself. The chart reflects reality: when it comes to birds, puppies not only know nothing—they don't suspect much, either. But once Sparky is in a position to start learning from his own experiences, the line on the chart becomes a function of an arithmetic progression. When he's finding birds because of the way he's hunting—that is, finding them on purpose—each one adds to the total, and eventually the dog becomes bird wise. Unlike the other cycles, it never turns downward.

The puppy that was Hazel looked back at me when I whistled, and I waved her in the direction the woodcock had taken. We started through a sunlit stand of aspens—popple, it's called in my part of the world. I listened to the puppy's bell as she covered the ground. The tip of her tail showed pink where she had caught it on one thorn too many. In a display of a trait that resembles both courage and stupidity, she continued to run beneath the thorn thickets, yipping in pain once in a while but hardly slowing. Someone would have to make a very good argument to convince me that puppies aren't having fun in the woods.

We had traveled a distance that I estimated to be one woodcock-flight when she abruptly slowed from "flat-out" to an "excited trot." Like all puppies, she always seemed slightly out of control in a jet-propelled way, so I knew something was up. I tried to get close to her before she could crowd the bird, but a once-flushed woodcock is wide awake, and this one wasn't going to hold still for my pup's subtle-as-a-locomotive tactics. He was up and gone in a moment. I fired a single shot into the air, paying homage to the idea of training.

The puppy hadn't seen the bird, and she stopped for a moment at my shot, wearing her "What's going on?" expression. She started toward me, but halfway in caught a whiff of the woodcock's body scent where he had been just moments before and instantly began her imitation of a runaway vacuum cleaner. I laughed.

Thankfully puppies are amusing, because at that stage of life any puppy has more faults than virtues. What they do have is a fast-forward energy that serves them well at this steep spot on their learning curve.

So, why all this information? If nothing else, the chart serves to pay the life cycles of a bird dog the compliment of acknowledgment. Conclusions are tough, but maybe what the chart shows more than anything else is what to expect. Consider the following:

There aren't too many positive things you can tell about a dog until he's well into his second year. The chart shows why. On the other hand, if you have a dog that's five and he isn't pointing birds, chances are he's never going to get any better. The chart illustrates that, too.

Train 'em early, because there is a great deal of truth in the old saw "You can't teach an old dog new tricks." The chart shows the cycle of a dog's receptiveness to training, and illustrates why, among other things, when training to retrieve is postponed until a time after the dog is steady to wing and shot (usually his third year), he may never fetch a bird.

Since breaking bad habits is a learning process, the chart also shows why a puppy should not be allowed to learn anything that he will have to unlearn later in life.

Although puppies can be taught things early on, don't push too hard until the puppy is nine months or so. He might not be ready for the training you want to give him.

Early in his life, a dog should run as much and as often as possible. (I have a puppy tearing up my back lawn on a daily basis as I write this.) Dogs develop their strength during the first couple years of their life, then ride it until time takes its toll.

I whistled to Hazel and waved her toward the corner where bittersweet tangles had climbed and overgrown the trees at the edge of the field. Instead, she cut back across the little clearing, then turned into the afternoon breeze and began working the cover toward the bittersweet corner. If I hadn't seen her make similar maneuvers several dozen times during the past month, I would have thought it was a coincidence. But there was no denying it: she had somehow learned to recognize good cover and then use the wind to work it properly.

And, somewhere along the way, she had also figured out that I couldn't smell.

At four, Hazel was no longer operating at the very edge of the laws of physics. While she still had the throttle wide open, I had noticed in recent months a tendency in her to avoid obstacles rather than blast right through them. She was becoming smart.

Some folks believe a bell on a bird dog serves to alert the bird. If we, the dog and I, were in every other way completely silent in the woods, it might be true. But as often as not, I find the bell distracts the bird and allows me to move up unnoticed. As Hazel approached the overgrown corner, I listened to the things her bell was telling me. Such listening is like the reluctant ballpoint pen that suddenly begins to write in the middle of a signature—afterwards, the unwritten part has more impact than the inked scribbles. When the bell stopped, I hurried toward the silence. My setter stood on a tentative point, her tail flagging. I whistled softly and she eased ahead and made one short cast before stopping abruptly in midstride. We were immediately in front of the bittersweet tangles now, and I circled wide to the wooded side and waited.

When I happened to look in the right spot, the bird was crouching close behind an angled boulder. As defiant as grouse seem when flushing, caught on the ground beneath a hunting dog's point there is nothing they resemble  *quite so much as a frightened chicken. No sooner had I seen him than the grouse must have figured the gig was up: in the blink of an eye he was in full flight, coming back at me through the hanging verticals. I wish I could report that I was cool enough to turn around and take an easy going-away shot, but I've got a bone in my head that won't let me do that. Instead, I took the bird station-8 style, and was lucky enough to almost miss him.*

Hazel brought the bird to me. An outsider looking in wouldn't be able to realize that she made the hard ones look easy. At four years old the dog had put it all together: her training was complete insofar as I could teach her. Now she was combining hunting tactics with an ever-growing body of knowledge about her quarry. She was strong enough to go all day long on every day she was called upon.

She was in her prime.

Expect very little in the dog's early years. A lot has to happen before a dog can become clever at handling birds. A dog needs time to develop hunt/search before he can acquire bird sense. Without hunt/search he won't ever find enough wild birds to learn what he must.

Years three through seven are the ones you should reserve to enjoy the fruits of your labors. That's all you get. Maybe what my father said about hunting goes for dog training as well: you have to love it, because the rewards are too fleeting to do it for any other reason.

If you have an addiction to pointing dogs, you might want to overlap their lives to insure you won't ever have to go cold turkey. Year seven is a good year to start a new puppy. That replacement will be blossoming into his own third year about the time your present dog falls off the end of the chart.

There is a house-that-Jack-built interrelationship between the five elements, with one being built upon another. There are positives from that process: a puppy exposed to the right imprinting will soak up the training you give him, and endurance permits hunt/search to develop, which, in turn, permits bird sense to grow and mature. But there are negative effects of this interrelationship, too. In later years as Sparky's endurance fails, hunt/search gets pulled down along with it. Ol' Sparky might know how he should cover his ground, but he just doesn't have the strength to do it any longer.

The chart might even explain "the sophomore slump." It exists among baseball players as well as bird dogs, and while I don't have any good explanation for why a rookie-of-the-year candidate will hit only .220 in his second season, there is an explanation why hunters are often disappointed in derby dogs.

You can see from the chart that a second year dog has doubled both his bird sense and hunt/search abilities, but there's still not much there—a nickel doubled is just a dime, after all. Yet his endurance is reaching a lifetime high. He is, in essence, a very fast car with lousy brakes and sloppy steering. Compared to what he will eventually become, he is just a slightly better dog than he was as a puppy.

Enter the human factor—Sparky is viewed much differently. In his sophomore year the things that were pleasant surprises last season are now expected as a matter of course. And the same mistakes that were so easily excused last year—he was "just a puppy," after all—become intolerable. In the mind of his owner, he's an experienced dog. In truth, he's a puppy with a year's experience. Be tolerant, and adjust your own thinking. Time will take care of the rest.

In dog training timing is, and always has been, of the essence. That was never a secret. To everything, including the life cycles of the complete bird dog, there is indeed a season.

Out of habit I whistled to Hazel, but she couldn't hear me. I waited, and just before she entered a grove of hemlocks she paused and looked back. I waved her to the right, and she turned and headed downhill.

At eleven, my deaf setter had learned to keep track of me in the woods. Amazing. During her prime, Hazel might have been the best bird dog in the state, but now most of her endurance had gone the way of her hearing, and I had taken to slipping half an aspirin into her food after each outing.

Hunting an old dog is a lot like playing catch with Whitey Ford or Jim Lomborg—today. It's not the same as it once was, but with a little imagination, it can almost be. The old girl didn't cover her ground as well, and certainly couldn't last as long as she did just two years before, but she did have a lifetime of bird sense going for her. And, like Lomborg and Ford, some wonderful history.

At the bottom of the hill Hazel glanced back at me again, and I waved her into the popples. We had been here together when the woodcock were so thick you could almost take them with a tennis racket. She began working scent almost immediately, and when she pointed it was a classic old dog's point: she nearly lay down.

I circled and walked toward where she told me the bird was. When I got there, a woodcock jumped up and headed for the open sky, knuckleballing through the near-leafless aspens. I tracked him to the top of his climb and when he folded he fell back through the branches. The old girl went to make the retrieve.

Dogs scent with their noses. I know that's not news, but it bears restating that when making a retrieve a dog carries the bird in a way that he has to breathe through the feathers of the bird being retrieved. I knew that, so I'm not sure if I ever really believed it was possible. But on this day I witnessed it for myself:

On her way back to me—with the woodcock in her mouth—Hazel swung around in midstride, took a half-dozen steps to her left and pointed a second bird.

I was flabbergasted.

What goes on when a dog scents a bird? I hope the answer always remains one of life's mysteries. Oh, dogs know, but I've never gotten one to tell me. Whatever that elusive process is, it's only raw data until the dog uses it. And some dogs use it far, far better than others. Bird sense is significantly more brains than nose. And, thank goodness, even though their physical abilities diminish, some dogs keep getting smarter as they go along.

I just wish I had a photo.

Sandy shook his head. "Well... You know me and field trials."

John considered his reply for a moment before he spoke.

"With you, I don't think your problem is so much with field trials as field trialers."

Sandy smiled, but said nothing.

Steven Mulak

"Meat Dog"

nine

Blue Ribbons
and
Red Tape

Amy slowed to an almost-point, still moving, but with the all-but-imperceptible speed of a clock's minute hand.

"Is that a point, Uncle Steve?"

"That's as good as you're going to get. She says there's a bird there but he's not holding still. Go see if you can make him fly."

Eric held his father's duck gun at port arms and marched in a series of looping circles. Nothing happened. He looked back at me and relaxed a bit when I waved Amy on. That was the exact moment the cock pheasant decided to jump from the weeds. Eric may have shot too quickly, but the bird tumbled. At the sound of the shot a second rooster jumped thirty yards away, and after a moment's hesitation Eric used the other barrel to put that bird down, too.

Amy brought in the far bird first, then spent some time rooting around before she came up with the wing-hit, too-close rooster that was Eric's first pheasant.

"Was that a double, Uncle Steve?"

"It was if you want it to be."

"No, really. Was it?"

"Technically, it was a 'report pair.' In my journals I call it a one-and-two. But no, it wasn't a double." I grinned and added, "But I'll tell your dad it was if you want me to."

Eric is a good kid—hardly a kid anymore, he was in his first year at the University of Maine when all this happened. To his credit he said, "No, I'll get a double on pheasants someday. A one-and-two sounds pretty good for now."

I took a photo of him with Amy and his first pheasants; then, since he didn't have a hunting vest, I put the birds in my gamebag. Amy dashed ahead when I whistled, and we started off.

"You've shot doubles, haven't you, Uncle Steve?"

I nodded.

"On grouse?" Eric knows the things that are most important to me.

"Well, legitimately just once, and even that was subject to cross-examination."

Eric gave me a questioning glance.

"In a full season, a hunter might see two grouse in the air simultaneously maybe three or four times. But just because two birds fly doesn't necessarily mean either one is shootable: bonafide opportunities for a double are rare. It took fifteen years before I finally connected. That was in 1985, I think. I was happy about it, and I put the incident in a story that *Sports Afield* ran."

Eric said, "Yeah, I remember that." He may be the only fan I have.

"A month or two later I got a letter from some guy—a writer. He wanted to know if the double was legitimate. Did the birds flush at the same instant? Hey, it was pretty well explained in the story: Hazel was on a walking point when a grouse flushed and doubled back off to the right, and when I went to pull on him the bird ended up being two birds. I shot 'em both. No problem.

"I got a second letter from this guy. He's got a quote from one of Burton Spiller's books: it's not a double unless I saw the birds take off, and they had to leave the ground at the same instant, he says." I shook my head. "That should have tipped me off. The guy was a crackpot.

"In the full context of the quote, Spiller was explaining to a young hunter that something like what you just did, Eric, is not a double. He explained to the kid that the birds have to come up together. Unfortunately, the exact words that Spiller wrote were 'at the same instant,' never thinking that fifty years later somebody was going to make an issue of phraseology.

"I know for sure that if the ghost of Burton Spiller himself had been there when I shot those grouse, he'd have been the first to congratulate me. It was a legit double by anyone's definition—except, of course, one chowderhead's. And me, I was fool enough to try to argue semantics with him."

By now, I was waving my arms around—or at least the one that wasn't carrying a shotgun. As I usually do when recounting what I've come to call "Le Affair d'Crackpot," I had succeeded in making myself angry. Eric said, "Don't let it bother you, Uncle Steve."

That was easy for him to say. He had two pheasants and a flunkie along to work the dog and carry the birds.

Semantics are an important part of every game. Frank Roach referred to one of the long-range Texas pointers we were hunting as a "county dog." In his time, Frank had judged some important field trials, so I thought it was a special term that I should know about.

"Well, in Texas field trialing," Frank explained, "We basically have three types of dogs: section, county, and state. When I say that Lady is a county dog, I mean she can be counted on to stay in the same county as her handler."

Frank, at times, could keep a straight face even after he was done pulling your leg. I never fell for that old trick. At least not the second time.

So much of what we enjoy in life hinges on definitions. Was it a nice brook trout or just a dace? Is that handsome 12-gauge a fine English gun, or a less-expensive Spanish model? Did the dog back the point on sight, or did she scent the bird and point on her own?

Definitions such as what exactly constitutes a bird dog's point are very important—but only in field trials. We shouldn't let definitions, particularly someone else's definitions, determine if we're having fun. I try not to anymore, but don't always succeed. Le Affair d'Crackpot can still get me going.

On a covey rise, my hunting partner dropped three quail with one shot—but it was with his second barrel. He missed completely with the first shot. Was it a triple? Well…its exact definition is only important in the semantical arena, and we weren't playing there at the time. He'll always remember when it happened, and he won't let me forget, and nobody else cares.

Did the dog point the bird, or just work it up? One of the attractions of hunting with bird dogs is that the most important rules are those you make for yourself. There are "sportsmen" out there who shoot birds on the ground. Me, I'd starve first. But I won't presume to apply my own set of rules to others.

That's just an opinion, but I thought it belonged here.

And those grouse flushed *together.*

Field trials are wonderful places not just to see bird dogs but to meet other people who like bird dogs. There is a method I use to initiate conversation with any dog person. It has never failed, since everyone who owns a dog has heard it before. I point to the person's dog and say, "Dusk yar dock baat?"

At times, I sound more like inspector Clouseau than Peter Sellers ever did.

Even away from their dogs, you can usually pick out dog people: their cars have roll-down tattoos—windows with dried dog drool all over them. In the summer, you'll notice that when a dog owner scratches a mosquito bite, his opposite leg will start tapping.

I met a stockbroker who tried to hide it. I really don't know why—maybe his boss didn't like animals—but he denied he owned a dog. He looked normal enough—a blue business suit without dog hair on the pantlegs and shiny shoes that had never stepped in something that had to be scraped off. I'll admit that for a while he had me fooled. But he spilled the beans when we went to lunch. As soon as he got up from his desk and started walking, his necktie got tangled under his front leg.

On my fortieth birthday, my wife gave me a set of golf clubs. I argued that I wasn't even six in dog years, but that didn't make a whole lot of difference to Father Time: my running days were over. Golf seemed like a pleasant way to pass a summer day, and if the truth be known, it is. Golf can be played alone. No one has to win or loose—you simply play and keep score if you want. The course itself provides the challenge. Played that way, golf is a mildly athletic noncompetitive pastime. Being a mildly athletic noncompetitive sort of guy, I enjoyed it.

At first.

Even in games like golf, competition can get so bound up in machismo that some men have a difficult time telling where enjoyment stops and pride takes over. I know, because it's happened to me. Tournaments. Teams. Leagues. Side bets. Handicaps. To tell the truth, winning really isn't all that important. It's losing that I hate. I guess competition has made me a better golfer. I work at the game now, and my handicap has come down steadily. But am I having as much fun as when I started? Next witness.

In many respects, bird hunting is like golf: you can do it alone, and you don't win or lose. But in their need to make a game of it, some hunters gravitate to sporting clays or skeet shooting. Others compete their bird dogs.

Essentially, field trials started with one fellow saying to another, "My dog's better than yours." The rest followed pretty much as you or I could have predicated it would.

It's easy to have fun at a field trial, and easy, too, to find yourself so bound up in that competitive thing that you don't have fun at all. I've entered my dogs in field trials and even won a few, and I've always considered it a compliment when I'm asked to be a judge. Once, back in the good old days, I took Winnie to a shoot-to-kill trial and cleaned house. Taking five pheasants as a bye sounded too much like a brag, so rather than talk about it I invented a noncompetitive character and put him in a story where his Brittany cleaned house at a field trial. The quote that opens the chapter is from that story.

Like golf, field trials can be a pleasant way to pass a sunny day in the company of pleasant people. It can easily be a game you play only for the sake of playing. But be careful—for some of us, the competitive bug is easy to catch and difficult to shake.

Competition and big money propel the cutting edge of progress. We duffers might still be playing with hickory-shafted golf clubs if it weren't for scientific improvements in equipment. Those improvements came about to answer the demands made not by recreational golfers, but by the pros who make their living driving a ball farther than the other guy. Similarly, just about every breed of bird dog has improved because of competition. During the last fifty years, English setters and Brittany spaniels, in particular, have been the beneficiaries of improvements that are the direct result of breeding dogs to field-trial standards. Pointers, unfortunately, might have become too hot for the amateur bird dog man to handle, although there are plenty out there doing the job. But any dog that is a "pointing fool" didn't get there by back-yard breeding.

Along that same line, I don't doubt that the shoot-to-retrieve field trials that are currently big in the Midwest are producing quality hunting dogs that a man might comfortably walk behind all day. That they will continue to do so is another thought. Just as auto racing created race cars, competitive dog contests tend to produce dogs that can win competitions. It's a form of evolution. Every field trial classification began as a way to compete one hunting dog against another, but soon evolved into contests between dogs that were bred and trained to the standards of that particular competition.

There was a time when I was so involved with the dog club that people had a tough time telling where I ended and the club began. *Want to sell a dog? Talk to Mulak— he's bound to know someone who's interested. Pointers? Steve knows a lot of pointer people. Dog food? Hey, Steve— who's that guy in the club who's a wholesaler?* Word spread like skin disease in a nudist colony. Without intending to, I had become the intermediary for all things vaguely canine.

I was signing up for a couple rounds of skeet when a fellow motioned for me to join him. "Hey, I would have called you last week, but I couldn't find your phone number. I need your help: my Brittany is in heat, and Smitty's dog must be too old—he just won't perform."

Smitty was there. He shook his head, ashamed. It was all his fault.

"She'll only be in for a few more days," the fellow continued. "And her next heat would be just before hunting season. I was hoping you could help me out."

For a moment I tried to look thoughtful. "Okay, but I've got three conditions. First, I'm not going to kiss her. Argue all you want, but I ain't gonna kiss no Brittany spaniel. Second, you gotta promise me that all the pups are gonna be raised Catholic. And third, I'll need a week to raise the money."

That, of course, was the punch line from an old joke about a gorilla and an Italian zookeeper, but it never went over any better. Even Smitty laughed.

Dog clubs, especially the nondenominational kind, can give you an overview of bird dogs in general, and offer a chance to see the good, the bad, and the ugly of several breeds. Years ago, when I was sure Brittanies were the only dog for me, I joined a bunch of local fellows who were starting a bird dog club. There were plenty of men with Brittanies in the club. Some were much worse than mine. But—and this was a shock—some were better. And a few were a lot better. I saw dozens of setters and dozens of shorthairs and dozens of Weimaraners. We even had some springers and a few guys with retrievers. Some dogs were well trained, others were runaways. Some were handsome and some were so ugly a man had to close one eye to look at them. And I saw pointers that hunted and pointed and retrieved, and looked good from the time they got out of the dog crate until they went back in. I was impressed. As a kid, not only had I never seen dogs like that, I hadn't even known of anyone who believed such dogs existed.

Back then I was absolutely certain that field trialing was to hunting what high-powered bass tournaments are to fishing. The stated purpose of the club was to promote the use of bird dogs. I nodded my head when I heard that, but I was too dumb to realize that "promoting bird dogs" pretty much means "field trials." Unfortunately we rapidly became what any sensible person despises about clubs. We became a group of fund-raisers, parliamentarians, and social meeting-goers. The main thrust of the club soon became its own internal workings.

But we did have a few fun trials. By way of definition, they were minor-league affairs: put your dog on a planted bird and win, at most, a ribbon. It gave us all a chance to look at one another's dogs and put our own in perspective.

Puppy events can be wonderful ways to see bird dogs as they really are. At that early stage of the game, training and experience cannot mask the dog's true essence. The list of things that one-year-old dogs are *not* is very long, but the one thing that can be said in their behalf is that they are perfectly genuine. More than at any other time of his life, you can make a pretty accurate assessment as to what sort of bird dog he will become.

I was never a very good puppy judge. I found myself always in the role of a fan, outwardly rooting for the dog. The most impressive of the lot was a happy young female pointer named Crystal. At barely twelve months old, she ranged like a good grouse dog and checked back every few minutes. Her owner, who was intent on turning her into something she wasn't, would yell at her.

"I've been told that she's a good dog," he said to me. "Don't you agree?"

I told him I did.

"Well, that makes one of us."

Whenever I wish I could go back in time, I'd like to go back to that one moment and get out my wallet and make an offer to buy that puppy. Few folks can agree on much of anything about bird dogs, except that the really good ones are rare. If you could have seen Crystal, you would have loaned me the money.

There are sports that are decided by the contestants. Objective sports, lets call them: you win by finishing the race before anyone else, or by hitting the other guy so hard he can't get back up. As often as not, a referee is hardly needed.

Then there are the subjective sports, those decided by the judges. An athlete might give the performance of his life, but when the judges hold up the numbers, there aren't enough 9.9s to beat the other guy. Virtually all sports have an element of each in their makeup, but field-trialing, unfortunately, lies far too much in the latter camp. Judges realize that and sincerely hope the best dog wins hands down.

There is an old saw that says the dogs place themselves, and for the most part that's exactly the way it happens: the dog you most want to take home is the one that gets the vote for winner. When the dogs cooperate, it's easy.

Where the hair-splitting starts is when judges recognize that a dog may be hunting rather than running, but is having an unlucky day and can't find birds. Another dog might blast through the whole course without ever breathing through his nose, then enter the bird field and have two finds. One dog hunted, one didn't. One was lucky, the other rolled snake eyes. Having to place one and not the other is like a choice between a rusty nail in the foot and the bulldog clap. Judges have nightmares over this sort of dilemma.

Every judge goes about placing a winner in his own way. When I've been asked to judge, my method is to break down a dog's performance into three categories: hunt/search, handling, and bird work. ("Hunt/search" is sometimes referred to as "run," but I would never get the two terms confused.) All are equally important. In turn, each dog is rated against all of the dogs that ran before it. One will have handled best, another second best, another third, and so on until one will have been the absolute worst. With three elements involved, it's conceivable that a dog might not be the best in any one particular area, but still might strike a good enough balance to be top dog. That would be my winner.

If you were judging with me, it would be up to me to convince you of that. Actually, the way we'd avoid a big argument at the end is to have a running series of small arguments as we went along, arriving at a "current standing" that we both agreed upon after each brace had run.

Field trialing is, of course, a game. Like other games, it has rules, and the game is won or lost by the rules. At some levels of competition the best bird dog in a field trial, the one who hunts joyfully and works the wind to a staunch point, is disqualified because his manners aren't up to snuff: he takes a few steps at flush, or ignores his bracemate's point. It's easy to look *only* at manners.

My rule in judging field trials is to allow the dog to put himself out of the trial. The dog should be judged on what he actually *did* rather than what he failed to do. In the world according to Mulak, sins of omission are excused, as are asinine plays by the dog's handler. That may seem overly generous, and as such there are a number of bird dog clubs that don't ask me to judge their trials anymore. But usually a dog that doesn't belong in the trial will provide the judge with plenty of reasons to rule him out, but you have to look for things other than just manners.

Too many folks think that if a dog runs like crazy and then points two birds, he should win the field trial. Not so. As a judge you must be prepared to justify your judgment, and not only to disinterested parties. A man who has spent an entry fee has a right to be told why his dog was not awarded a placement. My best advice is to be prepared. Confine your remarks to what the dog did or didn't do in relation to the rest of the field. Be truthful, be merciless, and be smart—don't volunteer anything unless asked, and that goes especially for the area of suggestions on how to improve.

It wasn't the first event I ever judged, but it was the first time I had a dilemma. It was a spring trial, and I was judging with Bill Puza, an old hand at the game. We met to discuss the previous brace. Neither dog had done much. I reported what I had seen: the dog—a young Brittany—had entered the water at the edge of the cattail swamp and apparently pointed near a wood-duck box. The handler had stomped out there and nearly drowned, but no bird flushed.

Bill asked, "Nothing?"

"Well," I said, "there was a duckling swimming around, but it never flew. Besides..."

Bill held up his hand. "Bird dogs are supposed to point live game birds and retrieve dead ones." he said. Then he offered an insight that I haven't forgotten to this day. Here's what he said: "Field trials are a joke."

We gave the dog third place.

I spent twenty-four years at sea, most of them as an engineer aboard a tanker. In that situation, you worked and lived alongside the same small bunch of people for two or three months at a time. Yet seldom did anyone ever know anyone else's real name. By that I mean men were often called by a nickname that was synonymous with their job: the radio operator might be Lawrence A. Easler, but there were a lot of blank stares if someone asked for Larry Easler. Aboard ship, his name was Sparks. And so was every other radio operator on every other ship anywhere.

The cooks were often Joe the Cook or sometimes Stew. The chief mate was always just Mate, and all pumpmen were universally called Pumps. There were chief stewards and chief pumpmen and chief mates, but the only guy aboard who was called Chief was the chief engineer, myself included. The other engineers and mates were either First, Second, or Third, depending on their ratings.

In special cases, a man had a nickname. There was a fellow named Listerine Eddie Callahan and another named Three-fingered Lawton. There was Scrap Iron Willinsky and Horseshit Harrington—not the sort of thing you'd want to holler across Grand Central Station or even the corner tavern, but names by which men knew other men, nonetheless. A particularly poor feeding cook, Arthur Paine, was, of course, called Hunger. A bald engineer was Skinhead Thompson, and Footsie Price was Footsie because of his shoe size. (Thank God he had the name before I got there.)

Of course, a different name appeared on the birth certificates of these fellows (usually the sort of first name that would make a man actually prefer being called Horseshit) but it didn't matter. Their names were Scrap Iron and Skinhead and Footsie, whether or not people actually called them that to their face.

(There was a woman named Beth Bradley who worked in the office. I never heard her called by that name. She was always Breath Badly. There was talk of getting her fixed up with Listerine Eddy, but it never worked out.)

Captains were into prestige. Properly, they were titled Ship's Master, and usually referred to themselves as such on the phone: "This is the master" or "This is Captain Swift." It was a disease, almost. As soon as a man was promoted to master, he'd call the phone company and have them change his name in the phone book to Captain So-and-so. We addressed them in person as Cap or sometimes Skipper, and referred to them by The Old Man, or more often simply their last name, although the less popular captains' names often carried a preceding adjective. Several were simply *that asshole*.

The chief engineer and the captain were on somewhat equal footing on the ship. That meant I was the only one who was in a position to punch holes in the old man's balloons, which could get over-inflated at the drop of an adjective. Supper was always a good time. We sat at opposite heads of the table, so everyone else was in on whatever transpired between us:

"You know, Cap, while I was home I had something happen to me that really got me to thinking."

"That's usually pretty dangerous for you, Chief."

The snickering from the supper eaters scored the first point for the old man, but I was setting him up. "Well, I've told you a bunch of stories about my bird dogs, but I'd have to say that the one best dog I ever saw was not one of mine but an English setter owned by Tom Lamica—a dog named Tekoa Mountain Chieftain. I judged that dog last year, and if ever there was a perfect bird dog, Ol' Chief was it. Eager and stylish, he would hunt, point, retrieve—everything but clean your birds for you."

The old man would nod almost as if he'd been listening. "Yeah, we've got some good ones back in Oklahoma, too..."

"Well, I was out hunting this past time home, and I ran into Tom Lamica in the woods. He had a beagle with him."

"A beagle?" That got his attention.

"Yeah. I couldn't figure it out either. I said to him, 'Tom, what are you doing with a rabbit hound? You own the best bird dog in New England in Old Tekoa Mountain Chieftan. What happened to him?' 'Well,' he said to me, 'two weeks ago I loaned him to Glenn Santos for a day. Biggest mistake I ever made.' 'Holy smokes!' I said. 'Did he accidently shoot him or something?' 'Naw, worse than that,' Tom said. 'He ruined a good dog on me. Half way through the hunt Glenn forgot Chief's name, and when he couldn't remember it he called him "Captain." The damn dog sat down and hasn't gotten off his ass since.'"

I ran that one by every skipper I ever sailed with. The supper table would laugh, albeit nervously. Sometimes—but only sometimes—so would the ship's master.

The world knows two types of fools: those who do not wish to climb Mount Fuji, and those who wish to climb it a second time.

Japanese proverb

t e n

Pointing Breeds and Breeding

I was late, nearly dark, when Duffy pointed. We had been heading back to the truck, skirting the field edge behind some farm buildings in Southampton. I assumed the buildings belonged to a farm, because of the chicken.

I approached his point cautiously, expecting a pheasant here in the open and not paying much attention to the piece of litter on the ground immediately in front of the dog's point. When nothing developed, I turned to wave my Brittany ahead. That's when I noticed that the white piece of paper was actually a chicken. She sat there among the weeds, wearing that silly startled expression that chickens affect, jerking her head spastically.

On his best day, Duffy was never a "broke" bird dog. If that chicken moved, it was going to be fly-or-die time. I put the gun down, got on all fours, and began to sneak up. Not on the chicken—hell, she wasn't the problem. No. I sneaked up on Duffy. I needed to collar the dog without giving the chicken reason to move.

I was almost within lunging distance when the chicken decided, on her own, to spaz-out. Lucky for her—unlucky for me—she ran at an angle that brought the dog within easy grasp of me as he charged forward. Now understand that this was 1973, and Duffy was in his prime. He was strong enough to pull me along the ground for twenty-five feet. I know that to be a fact because he did.

It was a close call, but the chicken escaped. During the remainder of his life, Duffy pointed virtually every species of game bird, waterfowl, and many of the reptiles native to New England. But never another chicken. And once the word on my heroics got around, I found it necessary to decline offers to enter rodeo bull riding competitions.

Enough is enough, after all.

When I was a kid my dad had Brittany spaniels—at least his last four dogs were Brits. He said they were good dogs. I loved my dad and never had reason to question his judgment. So, of course, when I bought my first dog (the above immortalized Duffy) it was a Brittany. Dad had Plymouths, so naturally I bought Chrysler products. He liked Poly-Chokes, so I liked Poly-Chokes. He carried his money in a billfold, so I did, too. He pitched horseshoes and drank Canadian whiskey rather than Scotch and favored pitch over poker, and so did I.

But as we live our own lives, we eventually grow away from some of those inherited preferences. When my Plymouth Duster rusted through after eighteen months, I bought a Chevy. I've become a cribbage player and I use double guns and I have a kennelful of setters (but I still have a billfold in my back pocket and a horseshoe pitch in my back yard, and Dad was right about VO, too).

Many of us have similar preferences—preferences accepted entirely on faith, inherited and adopted without trial. Does anyone ever use enough guns or boots or dogs to develop a truly objective opinion on the subject? You don't have to be an expert to know what you like, but most of us don't live long enough to know even that.

Here's a hunter just letting his dog out of the crate. Ask him what's the best breed of bird dog. If that's a Brittany running around at his feet, what are the chances he's going to tell you German shorthairs are best? About the same as finding an Indian-head penny in your change.

Compounding it all is Newton's eleventh law of momentum, often called the Buick axiom: "When the need for a new car arises, a man who has owned a succession of Buicks and has never had a problem with a Buick is not likely to buy any car that does not have holes in the side."

I've listened to men argue the qualities of pointers over setters, but I've never yet been present when anyone has actually won such an argument. (Wouldn't that be something: "You know, Elmer, I can see you're right. I'm going to shoot Ol' Sparky as soon as I get home, and I'll stop on the way and buy a pointer. Thanks for your help.") An articulate person would call such an argument "specious," but I don't. I call it rearranging deck chairs on the Titanic.

You've heard these arguments:

German shorthair pointers are the wrong color. So are Weimaraners, vizslas, and wirehairs. In the shadows, they're tough to follow as they move, and at times seem camouflaged. And you and I would have to agree. It's true.

Similarly, pointers and English setters are the wrong color. In the snow, they can be nearly impossible to see on point. And again, we'd have to agree. My white dogs can disappear when there's snow on the ground.

Okay. But Brittanies are the wrong color. If you don't believe that, hunt a Brit sometime in birch woods. Or patchy snow.

The truth is, it doesn't matter. Put a florescent collar on the dog. Even if he's invisible, it's a problem that can be overcome. Females come into heat. English setters and Brittanies have feathering that picks up burs. Males can be tougher to train than females. None of those are reasons for anything, just problems for which there are solutions.

Genuine hard information about the qualities and defects of a particular breed of bird dog are tough to come by. Go ahead, read a book about dogs. Each breed is described in glowing terms: "easily trained, loyal and loving, affectionate, intelligent, with boundless energy and a merry disposition."

Bull.

It's like reading your horoscope—there's no real information. What ever happened to expert opinion? The kind that says, "This is good, but those are as useful as the third man on a four-man bobsled team." Give me hard facts. If I buy a Lapland spaniel rather than a Australian pointing longhair, will he find more birds? Will he be easier to train? What bad habits will he have? Can he hunt when it's hot? How about when it's cold? How much does he shed? Can he drive on long trips? Will he eat kids and postmen?

There are a lot of different breeds out there. You and I have legitimate questions. There have to be differences. Why can't we get information like that?

I'll tell you why.

Your dog is going to look like others of his breed. After that, the really important differences have nothing to do with breed, but with breeding. He's going to be many of the same things his parents were. The individual traits passed on by his parents have much, much more bearing on how the dog turns out than whether or not he's of a particular breed. I've owned five English setters, and the specific differences from one to another were far greater than the general differences between, say, pointers and Brittanies. Some of my setters ran as they hunted, others trotted. Some trained easily, some were hardheads. Some were all-day hunters, others pooped out after three hours. Some were intelligent, others seemed barely smarter than me. Setters are supposed to be affectionate, people-loving dogs. Some of mine were, but if Amy doesn't think there's a chance you'll take her hunting, you don't exist.

So is one particular breed of dog more suited for you than another? Absolutely. If you're going hunting for birds, don't bring a Chihuahua. I consider that sound advice. Further, if you want your birds pointed, be sure to start with a dog that's from a breed that points. After that, good luck.

Having said that, I should say something about the idea that just because a dog might be of a pointing breed, that does not necessarily mean he's a *hunting dog*. What has been done to the Irish setter is legend. The pet store at the mall sells bird dog puppies mostly because they're cute, not because they're going to be hunting dogs. Even within the breeds, there are strains that have been bred as show dogs at the expense of their hunting instincts. There's nothing purposely wrong with them. It's possible they could become good hunters. But if I had to bet on a bird dog—and when you buy a puppy that's just what you're doing—I'd put my money on one whose parents were field rather than bench champions.

In a search for individuality, men will do a number of strange things, not the least of which involves owning things that nobody else has even heard of. When the road is full of Fords and Chevys, some men need to drive Hillmans and Citroens, not because they're any better, but just because nobody else does. Similarly, men pay a great deal of money for Latvian curly-coat spaniels or pointing pomeranians when people are trying to give away good English setters and Brittanies. Some of us have a continuing need to prove something to someone, and usually we know neither what that something is or who that someone might be. I don't understand it, but then again, there is much in life that falls into that category.

Don't get me wrong, I don't want to pretend that we can't like a breed because of the way dogs look or move or point. Some men are in love with "style," and have a kennelful of English pointers for that reason alone. Others are in love with the way red setters or Gordons look. Some breeds don't have tails, and that's a sticking point with some folks. Some dogs are known to howl instead of bark, and I've heard men say unrepeatable things about that trait. My wife thinks all short-coated male dogs should be made to wear jockstraps. Who am I to argue?

The fact that I like English setters is nothing I'd want to base an argument on. Hazel's mother was the most biddable dog I had ever judged, so when Bill Puza bred to her I took one of the puppies. I bought my other setters partially because of the Buick axiom and partially in the hopes of getting Hazel again.

Colonel Paul, who I introduced to you earlier as Rusty's owner, was at the house for my annual woodcock feed. He looked out at the kennel and saw that among my own setters was a German shorthair. I was training her for a fellow. Colonel Paul is the sort of guy that you wish was your uncle, even after you've grown up. He has spent a lifetime hunting behind bird dogs of his own making. That those dogs were always the envy of other hunters says a lot more about his abilities as a dog trainer than he ever would. "Be careful," he advised me. "Those Continental breeds will spoil you. They train easy and well."

He was right.

Nature has a way of getting people to take care of all the dogs of the world: she starts them off as puppies. They piddle on the floor and chew the legs of the table you just had refinished, but they get away with it because they're puppies. Mother Nature knew what she was doing when she made them cute.

There was a pumpman from Maine who joined the ship I was on. To say he was quiet was like saying Amelda Marcos had a few pair of shoes. He was on the ship for a week before I ever heard him say anything, and I was the chief engineer—he was supposed to be working for me. Over his workbench he had a photo of his wife, himself, and their big-as-a-desk Saint Bernard. I figured he was a dog lover, and used that to get him talking.

He told me that if his wife ever left him and he needed to start meeting women again, he would go out and buy a Saint Bernard puppy just like the one his dog had been and take it with him wherever he went. Women, he told me, couldn't help themselves: they'd walk up to him on the street, stop their cars as they were driving by, even walk away from their boyfriends—just so they could pet that absolutely drop-dead adorable puppy. He added that as soon the dog got to be about six months old, his plan was to shoot the damn thing and start over again with another five-week-old Saint Bernard.

He told me all this with a straight face. At least I assume he kept a straight face—I was busy taking notes at the time.

"How to pick a puppy" is a great topic for all sorts of dissertations. Some men will assure you that the most aggressive puppy in the litter will be the "best" dog. Others will guarantee that that one will be the most hardheaded. Both may be right.

There used to be a TV commercial—I've long since forgotten what they were selling—that showed people and their dogs walking by. A tall lanky long-haired blond had an equally tall and lanky Afghan hound, and a tough-looking jowly fellow had an English bulldog. The idea, of course, is that people often resemble their dogs. But is it that people resemble their dogs, or that they choose dogs which conform to the image they have of themselves?

I know a man who picks out a puppy by taking on the whole litter in a fistfight. Really, he gets down on all fours and starts smacking the pups. Hostilities continue to elevate until only one dog remains to answer the bell for the next round. That's the dog he buys. His explanation? "I want a dog that's just like me." (Understand, the guy is nearly fifty, but he recently had his arm broken in a bar fight.)

I don't really have a lot of expertise in puppy picking. When I showed up at Bill Puza's to look over his five-week-old puppies, I had my daughter with me. This was 1978, so she was just seven at the time. Of the six females, none looked any more promising than the rest. What can anyone tell at five weeks? White dogs, black spots. One of them came to the edge of the table to sniff at Jennifer's hand. Bill moved them around, shuffling the deck, talking all the while of markings and conformation. I had made Jennifer promise not to say anything, and she didn't. But twice the little hand sniffer crawled over her litter mates for another visit to Jennifer. I think you can guess the rest of the story. That was Hazel. You can see why I tell people she picked us.

Since then I've picked out four puppies for myself and three for other people, and the Jennifer theory has proved its worth; I take the puppy that likes me best. Some men would argue that that doesn't say much for the IQ of the puppies I pick, but what do those men know?

I should say something about the fact that there are several serious puppy-picking systems based in good science. They assign a point value to various responses the puppy might make to being handled or having a bird wing thrown around. These systems sound convincing. But puppies are just like babies. There's not a lot you're going to be able to tell with any certainty. In reality, you pick the sire and dam, and take a chance on the puppy you choose from the litter.

In an age where mild profanity is all but universal, I've adopted Groucho Marx's favorite derogatory term. I call certain people chowderheads. People often ask me just what exactly a chowderhead is. Actually, no one ever asked me that, but if they did, this would be my answer:

The best Brittanies I've ever seen anywhere belonged to a fellow I barely knew. His dog Doc was hunting and pointing staunchly at an age when other puppies were still trying to figure which way was up, and Doc continued to be an outstanding performer as he matured.

After a dog club meeting one night, we were in a bar talking to a new guy. He owned a female Brit he wanted to breed. Everybody at the table told him about Doc—we had all been impressed by that dog at one time or another. Doc was it. But the new guy, who up until then didn't seem like an escapee from the Sunday funnies, was only was interested in finding out how big Doc was.

He's not big. He's about thirty-five or forty pounds—a standard-size Brittany.

No, he won't do. The new guy wanted big. He was intent on doing for dog breeding what Dom DeLuise has done for pole-vaulting. Never mind that Doc is the kind of dog some men would trade their first-born son for. The new guy is on a mission to breed giant Brittanies.

And that, folks, is what a chowderhead is.

The Plains Indians were the most successful horse breeders the world has ever seen. They consistently bred ponies that could outrun the best that the United States Cavalry could send after them. They did it by breeding for a single trait—speed. Never mind what he looked like, how big he was, what his disposition was. Never mind that he belonged to the chief's brother-in-law, or that he could add and subtract with his hoofs. Could he run? That was always the only question. It's safe to say they would have bred to Doc and used the new guy as coyote bait.

The chowderhead factor aside, men get involved in doing their own breeding because they hope the pups will inherit whatever it is they like about Ol' Sparky. But, unfortunately, one only breeds dogs—one doesn't clone them. Since you can't keep track of all the pups, you'll never know if the one that the sweet old lady bought for her daughter in Springfield was *the one*.

For all the trouble and expense of back-yard breeding (it's a mistake to think in terms of making or saving money—it never works out, no matter how you figure it) there has to be an element of recreation involved. We are amateurs, remember. And while I can understand why a man would want to breed his dog, it's tough to fathom why he would go through it all a second time. A friend of mine tried it. Once. I've heard him say this more than a few times, so I believe it's true: "No matter how much fun it might be, it all goes down the crapper the first time you step in puppy shit with your bare feet."

When it comes to dog breeding, I am and intend to remain a customer. My female dogs are spayed. I've made good dogs out of puppies that other men have bred, and believe I can continue to do so in the future. That means I go shopping.

"These are grouse dogs," the breeder told me. "The sire was a grouse champion at three years old and so was the dam, so the puppies should be grouse dogs, too."

Hey, that sounds convincing to me.

But look a little further. Consider for a moment the premise that any bird dog can learn to hunt grouse if given enough training. If I had been *smart* (something I've only been sarcastically called) I should have asked: How many encounters with a grouse did it take to make the father a grouse dog? A hundred? Five hundred? A thousand?

If the breeder lives in the backwoods of Minnesota, putting any dog on a thousand grouse during the first three years of its life might not be very difficult. On the other hand, if it takes a thousand grouse to make young Sparky a grouse dog and you live in suburban New England, you might not see that many birds in *your* lifetime, let alone the dog's.

No. A good bird dog has to be one whose breeding and temperament predispose him toward being receptive to training. Then, given enough experience on wild birds, he stands a good chance of becoming a grouse dog. Or a quail dog. Or a pheasant dog. Or whatever it is that the breeder is advertising his dogs to be.

Puppies, let's face it, are not their parents. The essence of the problem is that dogs are complex creatures that are bred one to another—there is no cloning involved. Breeders who would tell you otherwise are doing their dogs a disservice.

If I could go back to that moment in time, I'd want to actually see the parents rather than just their achievements. Do they hunt in a manner that I can live with? Are they biddable? Easily trained? Do they have a history of passing those good traits on to their pups? And then, with my eyes wide open, I'd take a chance that the puppy I picked out would carry those same traits.

You never know. Maybe even I could turn him into a grouse dog.

Dogs are all of the same species. While they might outwardly look vastly different from breed to breed, they are, all of them, still dogs. As such, there really isn't a great deal of difference between a mastiff and a 'toy poodle—much less than between a fox and a wolf, for instance.

In *Wing & Shot* Robert Wehle addresses a problem in breeding called "drag of the race." It's a tendency for the extraordinary to revert toward the average. He uses a hypothetical example of fifty Great Danes left to themselves on an island. After just a few generations without the influence of man, the drag of the race would have negated all the traits that make Great Danes Great Danes. The dogs would have reverted to a common type that resembles the mongrel who lifts his leg on the corner mailbox each morning at the end of my street.

Animals don't get much more extraordinary and specialized than pointing dogs. Wehle makes a case for line breeding and inbreeding as methods of promoting those extraordinary characteristics. A case can also be made for the Plains Indians' method. I don't know a lot about genetics and bloodlines, so I'm easily snowed by such talk. I can't win that game, so I don't play.

Instead, I want to know that the guy I'm buying the puppy from believes in what he's doing and is interested enough to pay attention to the results. Every detail of how to make a good bird dog may be figured out someday, but don't bet on it. In the end, you pays your money and you takes your chances. I just want to be sure the chance I'm taking is on the dog, not the breeder.

My daughters (little girls then) named the dog Winnie, and once in a while I called her that. But she was a pet as well as a hunting dog, and also answered to Winn, Win-Bin, Ninnie Girl, Nit-Bit, Nitch-ka, Nacheeka, Winsor, and Bird Brain. The advice I offered about avoiding names that sound alike or have similar endings all comes to nothing in light of the above confession. If you're like the rest of us, whatever you name you dog doesn't matter because, as often as not, you'll call him something else. That should be comforting to anyone who spends any amount of time mulling over names, searching for the exact right one. Hard cheese for the advocates of reason.

A hunting partner owned a Ryman English setter named Tweed. Whenever we'd hunt together and he'd call his dog, somehow I'd hear my name. Now, understand that my hearing is long overdue for its 100,000-mile overhaul. He used to make less-than-funny jokes about my not handling well, but at least coming when called.

Another friend believes in one-syllable, forceful names: Brit, Zee, Cue. He's got a lot of good reasons, and he all but had me convinced that I should do the same. Until I noticed that in nonhunting situations his wirehair became "Cue-cue." I was shattered. It was the same sort of disappointment I had in finding out that Mister Ed's lines were dubbed.

Lately I've named my dogs after my aunts. I like those old, out-of-fashion names. But if ever there were a reason to have just one litter of puppies, it would be so that I could give them names. I'd call them Fido and Rover and Spot and Duke and, of course, if I really liked one more than the others, I'd call him Sparky.

We were at the ASPCA. This was so long ago that I don't even remember what we were doing there, but Susan and I were sitting in the waiting area with whichever dog we had at the time, waiting to go in and see the vet.

A fat woman came through the door carrying a box of puppies. I'm not sure if they were of any breed at all. There were a bunch of them, and they must have been five or six weeks old because they had already eaten half of the cardboard box. They bounced around and wrestled with each other, nearly spilling the box every so often, yipping and playing as only puppies can.

For her part, the woman was so fat I swear I could hear tuba music playing as she walked. It appeared that she had awakened and come directly to the animal hospital. She had on a pair of rubber shower shoes and a house dress that looked like she had slept in it, and her hair looked about the same. This must have been during hunting season, because against the chill the fat woman had thrown on what remained of a woolen buffalo plaid shirt. If it belonged to her husband, he was a size XXL—maybe three Xs. The back of it, the shirt tails and one of the sleeves had been torn to shreds, and bits of green and black wool hung like fringe from the edges.

One of the volunteers approached her. "I wanna give you these puppies for adoption," the woman said. She heaved the box up onto the counter. "I can't take care of 'em no more."

There was a murmured reply from the volunteer, but I couldn't hear what transpired because Susan was whispering in my good ear. Understand that my wife would be at home on the range: I seldom hear a discouraging word from her. But not this time. She said, "I'll bet the next time those puppies poop, it'll be green plaid."

In an earlier chapter, I compared a puppy to a package of tomato seeds, with the gist being that just because both might come from well-bred stock, they each need proper care and nurturing if they are to bear fruit. But there is another comparison that any gardener realizes is equally accurate. Whatever the cost of the seed itself—from the cheapest supermarket packets to the most expensive hybrid varieties—whatever the expense, it's nothing compared to the cost in time, labor, and actual dollars that goes into producing the finished product.

Dogs are like that. Lately, well-bred English setter puppies bring $400. But by the time you pay for shots and licenses and registration; a lifetime's worth of dog food and vet bills, then all the collars, bells, leashes, and combs; the cost of a dog kennel or a fence around the yard, the shoes and gloves and furniture legs they chew up, plus the hugely incalculable time and effort that goes into training any dog—by the time you pay for all of that, the initial cost of a puppy, whether he's a dog pound mutt or a line-bred scion of champions, is little more than a drop in the bucket. (The vet bills alone over the average dog's lifetime comes to an amount slightly less than it takes to buy a private airplane.)

The dog, and the return you get from owning him, is something most men could not put a price on. For some it's a burden. For others, a priceless joy. But one thing is sure: "It's gonna cost ya."

In November, there are lovely outings when it seems a hunter walks from one calendar picture into another and the day goes by like a melody—wonderful days that seem to glow with their own luminescence. When any of us looks forward to autumn, these are the days that immediately come into focus in the mind's eye. But, as I'm sure you know, there are other days when the rosy hue is absent. There is no such thing as a "pleasant November rain," at least not on my side of the Mason-Dixon line.

It was a day like that, only worse. I was cold and wet, and my fingers were numb. The highlight of the day had come moments before when I got back into the truck and opened the thermos and caught the aroma of hot coffee.

On the floor of the truck, an eight-month-old puppy named Sophie sat shivering—far more with excitement than from the cold rain that had soaked her to the skin. During the past two hours afield she had bumped birds and gotten scolded and, at one juncture, she had been chased down by a big angry wet guy with a penchant for hauling her around by the ear. Yet she sat with her engine on fast idle, yelping quietly every few moments, eager to get going again.

I changed into my spare sweater. *Maybe an hour more.* Was that me thinking that! This is crazy. Really, what am I doing out in this weather?

The dog looked up at me, waiting not altogether patiently. She was all that a puppy should be. Spirit and raw, heedless vitality. Her first point still lay somewhere in the future, but we were getting closer to it all the time. Her tail thumped against the door.

I should write a book.